1

GAS

AT $1.25 PER GALLON

How We Get There in Six Weeks

THE FIRST STEP

TOWARD TRUE

ECONOMIC RECOVERY

First published digitally June 2013 by Bob Rice

First published in print in December of 2013 by Bob Rice using Create Space

ISBN-13: 978-1491298466 (Create Space Assigned)
ISBN-10: 1491298464

To my devoted wife Paulette

And my children Joe and Amy

ACKNOWLEDGMENTS

This book was authored and edited by Bob Rice. During this months-long process, I am deeply grateful for the sacrifice incurred and help provided by my dear wife Paulette. She typed (and retyped) legible versions of the manuscript as I dictated my hand written copy to her. She also navigated the tedious process of uploading and converting the manuscript to a suitable Create Space file.

In attempting to self-publish a book, a rough working knowledge of the process is required. Examples would include an understanding of copyright issues, fair use guidelines, publishing formats, browsing categories, file uploading requirements, keywords, BISAC codes, ISBN numbers to mention a few.

Thus, our heartfelt thanks go out to several people, typically bloggers and authors, whose various internet posts helped us to better understand the process. Included in this group are David Carnoy (CNET) Dean Fetzer (Gunboss), Jane Friedman, Louisa Locke, Rafe Needleman (CNET), and Lonnie Rosenbaum from Ganxy. In addition, we thank the various individuals from Create Space whose telephone correspondence with us regarding reformatting, uploading and other issues were very helpful. Ditto: various graphic designers available online through the company, Fiverr.

TABLE OF CONTENTS

PART III: TOWARD A REAL ECONOMIC RECOVERY

INTRODUCTION

FIRST...A COUPLE OF QUESTIONS

So, why have I written this book? The short answer is "to inform"... and promote change. More specifically, the Federal government of the United States of America, beginning at the turn of this century and continuing even today, has successfully (in my opinion) hustled hundreds of millions of its citizens. Economically speaking, it is perhaps the most successful job in recent American history of Federal government policy makers hoodwinking virtually the entire electorate.

At any point during the past 13 years, you could have asked two different Presidents, a vast majority of Congressional members or various other high level Federal government employees this question. Is there anything you can do about what seems to be artificially high fuel prices? Almost unanimously, their answer would be something along these lines, "unfortunately there is nothing we can do in 'the short run' to dramatically bring down fuel prices." My position is that such responses are either naive or disingenuous.

In the chapters that follow, I will make the case that the federal government has actually promoted (not discouraged) higher fuel prices in America during the past thirteen years. More importantly, I will describe and promote a simple, straightforward plan that would in effect allow free market forces of supply and demand to quickly and dramatically reduce artificially high crude oil prices, which would then result in rapidly falling gasoline and other fuel prices. Lower gas prices would increase disposable income for millions of families nationwide. This extra (widespread) disposable income would then be spent primarily at local businesses, which, I argue, would ignite a true widespread economic recovery (as detailed in Chapter Seven).

SECOND QUESTION: WHAT ABOUT QUALIFICATIONS?

The original question begs a second question. Why would I, a pretty average human being, be qualified to write this book? The easy answer is that I am qualified "by default". Apparently, no one else on the planet has seen fit to write a book describing how to quickly bring down crude oil and gas prices, thereby igniting a widespread economic recovery.

A more specific answer is this. For over 35 years, as explained later, I have been "hyper-focused" on the ever changing worldwide price of crude oil which, of course, is the primary cost factor in the production of gasoline. Artificially high crude oil prices virtually always produce artificially high gasoline prices.

Following the trend of the previous hundred plus years of crude oil production, the average price of a barrel of crude oil during most of the 1980's and virtually all of the 1990's was relatively cheap. The ever changing world wide price of a barrel of crude oil during this time period was roughly $15 to $25 per barrel, with the price occasionally falling as low as $8 per barrel. Not surprisingly, the price of gasoline during the 1980's and 1990's was typically quite low. In metro Atlanta, prices averaged around 75 to 80 cents per gallon for regular gasoline.

Then something happened. Beginning early in this century, the price of crude oil (and thus, the price of gasoline) began to rise. Within a few years (and continuing even today), Americans found themselves paying three, four or even five times more for a gallon of gas than they had paid, for example, during January of 1999.

As a long time retailer (and ever focused on oil prices), I recognized early on that a serious lack of competition was now occurring in the production and sale of crude oil and gasoline. After all, prices for crude oil had increased five-fold during the first five years of the 21st century...with no apparent shortage of crude oil anywhere. (Except for the short period after Hurricane Katrina, do you remember a time during the past 13 years that your favorite local gas station had no gasoline to sell?)

Eventually, I did a little research and quickly came to understand the relatively simple reason why crude oil and fuel prices were artificially high. Similarly, I quickly recognized how easy it would be "to bring down" such artificially high gas prices.

As the years went by, I was amazed (and angered) that no influential politician, economist, government regulator or media pundit was making the obvious case for quickly bringing down fuel prices. To me, the continued existence of artificially high fuel prices has always been akin to the proverbial dead elephant across from the punch bowl at the party.

Indeed, artificially high fuel prices seemed destined to become "the new normal"...unless someone "set the record straight". By default, that someone apparently has to be me. Shortly after I became semi-retired (and had more time), I began writing this self-edited, self-published, "long shot effort" to bring down fuel prices.

A LITTLE BACKGROUND...AND THE 100 FOOT HIGH WALL

For 32 years, my wife and I owned and operated retail stores in the metro Atlanta area, at one point owning six business locations. Then, a little more than four years ago, we closed our last retail location when the lease expired.

The primary reason we closed the store in 2009 was not the financial crisis of 2007 and 2008, but rather it was because of ever increasing and unstable gasoline prices, beginning in 2001 and of course escalating between 2005 and 2008. Our business model was particularly dependent on low gas prices, but no doubt, many other marginally profitable small businesses and restaurants, all of whom are continually buying merchandise or food to resell, were also hammered by ever higher fuel prices. Even more important, millions of "potential" middle class customers were now being drained of disposable income as they spent $50 to $80 filling their gas tanks that required only $15 to $20 for a fill up, during most of the 1980's and virtually all of the 1990's.

During 2007 and 2008, I wrote several different articles outlining an approach; that is, a plan which would quite possibly have allowed Congressional members the opportunity to very quickly bring down the price of gasoline. I called various Congressional offices and talked to Congressional staff members explaining my ideas. I also sent copies of the articles to various newspapers and other publications.

During these efforts, my position was, "can you simply talk about it; that is, debate the plan on the Congressional floor? See what the public in turn thinks about the proposal." My feeling, back then, was that Congressional members (and media types) would recognize that the plan (to quickly reduce fuel prices) had, at the very least, "some potential" for economically aiding struggling middle class Americans...and would subsequently be debated and publicized.

Despite many hours of effort, I failed to gain any meaningful publicity for the plan (to quickly bring down fuel prices). I simply could not penetrate the "protective wall" surrounding those who were economically or otherwise benefitting from high fuel prices. (I did have one short 450 word article published on the website of "The Hill" newspaper in Washington DC, but conveniently enough, Congress was out of session at the time).

FIVE YEARS LATER...AND NOW MORE EXPERIENCED

Now five years later, being semi-retired, drawing Social Security and enrolled in Medicare, high gas prices have much less impact on my wife and I. Still, as gas prices continue to be unstable and artificially high, I empathize with the business owners trying to "hang on" and also for the tens of millions of working Americans living frequently from paycheck to paycheck. I would like to help these folks...and "bore through" the protective wall mentioned above. If you would like to join me (be ye Republican or Democrat) and be part of an effort to bring gas prices down to perhaps as low as $1.25 per gallon during the next several months, then please read and seriously consider the relatively simple solution that I outline in the following chapters.

As noted above, similar efforts on my part in 2007 and 2008 to bring down gas prices failed. However, the personal experience gained from those years has given me a better idea of "how the game is played" in Washington DC and beyond. It goes something like this:

GAME PLAN FOR DC POLITICIANS... AND MEDIA PUNDITS

<u>All</u> politicians claim to have an undying allegiance to the economic welfare of middle class citizens (and of course, small business owners). This concern is real. The economic well-being of the middle class citizenry hugely impacts who gets re-elected. Unfortunately, most politicians also feel

they <u>must</u> have the financial support of wealthy citizens and generous special interest groups. Conventional wisdom dictates that winning re-election in America requires a lot of money; that is, it typically requires contributions from many especially generous campaign donors.

Thus, Presidents and Congressional members, Democrats and Republicans alike, (as well as their defenders in the media) spend a goodly amount of time contemplating and implementing strategies or policies to keep both groups of individuals (that is, middle class citizens and wealthy campaign contributors) happy. The simplest and most used approach by these Federal politicians is to simply "ignore", if possible, potential legislation which could benefit the middle class, if that same legislation might in fact put frowns on the faces of large campaign donors. (Such shenanigans in the halls of Congress are discussed in more detail in the book's last chapter entitled, "Congress: Will They Cooperate?".)

Similarly, many media outlets (for example, newspapers) will sometimes refuse to print a decent article with unique ideas that could economically help middle class families, because major newspaper advertisers (or multi-millionaire newspaper owners) might be adversely affected by the publicity generated by such printed articles. (It is interesting that Americans, like the citizens of most true democracies, are constitutionally protected from censorship or other undue influence of the Federal government regarding the media. However, Americans have virtually no such protections from individuals and companies that might "privately" censor, control, or otherwise influence what is reported in the media. Understand that "a handful" of individuals and companies in recent years have been allowed to take control of the vast majority of major media outlets in America.)

NO GUARANTEES...
BUT A NEW APPROACH

So now, in 2013, I clearly understand that many, many, many politicians will deliberately ignore, when possible, legislation that could economically help the middle class. Also, I clearly understand the potential bias (as described above) of high powered decision makers at media outlets, when it comes to deciding what gets printed, heard, seen or otherwise aired. Thus, I am using a different approach this time around.

In 2007 and 2008, my primary efforts focused on writing various "articles" and "hoping" that they would be published or publicized via Congressional debate. This time (in 2013) I have written a book, which has been published. The "potential" for publicity cannot be denied. I simply have to convince you to read the book and help me publicize its simple plan to quickly bring down fuel prices; force "dodging and weaving" politicians to take a stand, one way or the other, regarding the book's plan.

PIPE DREAMS...AND ECONOMIC RECOVERIES

Despite my assurances, I understand that for many of you, the prospect of gasoline for less than a $1.50 per gallon by next month, seems like a pipe dream. However, I would not have spent well over a thousand hours writing this book if I did not sincerely believe that such prices can become a reality.

So, the immediate goal of this book is $1.25 per gallon gas, by next month. However, as you read, it should become obvious that achieving this goal would not simply save us money at the gas pump. It would also reflect a major "change in progress", regarding how Federal politicians in Washington come to view the government's role in helping to implement a "widespread" economic recovery in America...one that actually includes middle class families and small business owners. Gasoline at less than $1.50 per gallon is an obvious way to ignite such an economic recovery (as described in detail in Chapter 7).

A BOOK...THAT IS EASY TO UNDERSTAND

My adult life has been spent in retail store management and many years of actually owning retail stores. I have a goodly amount of writing experience, but I am not, of course, a professional writer. This self-edited book was never intended to be an academically applauded literary work. Accusations of "proof by assertion" (a "no-no" in the literary world) are perhaps valid.

There are no, or very few, acknowledgments, references, works cited, footnotes, etc. Graphs, charts and timelines are not included.

Rather this book, more than anything else, is a collection of personal observations and personal solutions which I think are frequently unique, yet ironically, once described, typically become "intuitively obvious to the casual observer (or reader)". If nothing else, this book should serve as "food for thought", offering the reader a new and different way to view the American political landscape and the "economic war" of sorts taking place within.

So, a parallel goal of the book is to describe the problems and solutions impacting the middle class in such a way that virtually anyone using common sense, can understand what is going on. This goal may prove to be a little annoying for a few readers who already have a good working knowledge of various situations that I try to make "absolutely clear".

"A CALL TO ACTION"…CAN YOU SPARE TEN MINUTES?

The solutions that I propose, to bring down gas prices and help bring about a widespread American economic recovery, require at least "a few minutes" of help from the reader. So in the end, this book is a "call to action". In other words, the book identifies problems, offers solutions and then challenges readers to help bring about change.

It is my hope, of course, that once readers come to realize the extent of the "economic shafting" of middle class Americans, that such readers will become more deeply involved…as they seek to force their four elected representatives in Washington to debate our proposals. These four elected representatives would be one member from the U.S. House of Representatives, two members from the U.S. Senate and the President.

Success may be a "long shot", but if we should succeed, then millions, if not billions of individuals will economically benefit in the days ahead. These tired idioms may apply, "there is no heavier burden than a great opportunity", or how about "if not us, then who…if not now, then when?"

WHAT TO EXPECT… IN CHAPTERS AHEAD

The ten chapters of the book are organized into three different sections. This three part break down of the book includes Part 1: Crude Oil Speculation, Part 2: Oil Company Competition and Part 3: Toward a Real Economic Recovery.

The book begins with an article that I wrote five years ago in 2008, entitled "Congress Hustles America", with only minor revisions having been made. It is interesting and saddening that the article is as relevant today as it was in 2008. The article focuses on the problem of "artificially" high fuel prices. In 2008, just as in recent months and years, prices for regular unleaded gas sometimes approach or surpass $3.50 per gallon in many parts of America. In addition to high and unstable gas prices, many of the economic problems facing "Main Street" in 2008 are still around in 2013. Some examples include:

An unprecedented demise in most of America's housing market

A lack of disposable income and credit throughout huge sectors of middle class America

The economic demise of middle class small business owners

College graduates who are either unemployed or under-employed, but with student loan debt often exceeding $30,000

Increasingly difficult access to affordable, quality health care coverage

PART ONE

CRUDE OIL SPECULATION

CHAPTER ONE

TWELVE YEARS OF HIGH GASOLINE PRICES: WHY?

When my wife and I opened our first retail store in 1977, the price of regular gas in the metro Atlanta area was roughly 80 cents per gallon. In early 1999, the price of gas was roughly 80 cents per gallon. During the vast majority of the months between 1977 and early 1999, the price of gas in metro Atlanta averaged around 80 cents per gallon.

However, early in this century, gas prices began to rise and become more unstable. During the past ten years, prices for regular gasoline in the Atlanta area have averaged above $3.00 per gallon for regular gasoline. In July of 2008, prices for regular gas in Atlanta rose to $4.25 per gallon. Currently (in December of 2013), regular gasoline in metro Atlanta sells for around $3.25 per gallon.

So, some of the questions to be answered in the following chapters are these:

Why have gas and other fuel prices become more unstable and trended generally much higher during the past twelve years of this century?

Is there a "genuine shortage" of crude oil during this century, compared with the supply available, for example, during the 1980's and 1990's, which in turn, has driven crude oil prices higher? (Remember, higher crude oil prices produce higher gasoline prices.)

Will crude oil producers continue indefinitely to receive $85 to $110 for a barrel of crude oil that sometimes costs them less than $20 per barrel to bring to the surface?

Will the Federal government, using the Federal Reserve, continue to promote artificially high prices for crude oil and gasoline by "magically" creating money known as Q.E. dollars and then pumping these dollars (currently 85 billion per month during 2013) into the bank accounts of investment bankers? (These bankers can subsequently use the Q.E. money to speculate, bet or otherwise bid up the ever-changing worldwide price of crude oil.)

Will middle class small business owners, less prosperous individuals, and middle class families simply have to learn to deal with widespread shortages of disposable income, created in part by high gas prices?

Are low gas prices "a thing of the past", while high and unstable gas prices are "here to stay"?

Or is it possible that higher fuel prices have causes that can be reversed? Is it possible that specific individuals, companies and government institutions are directly or indirectly responsible for higher and unstable gas prices and are subsequently benefitting economically from such artificially high fuel prices? Is it possible that we, acting together, can overcome the forces promoting inflated fuel prices?

In 2007 and 2008, I wrote five different articles that I posted on the internet, sent to newspapers or emailed to Congressional politicians. These articles were a futile attempt to publicize what I considered to be illegitimately high and unstable gas prices, and a solution to deal with the problem.

The following article, entitled "Congress Hustles America", is one of the five articles that I wrote. Unfortunately, the article is as relevant in December of 2013 as it was five years ago. I have only slightly modified the article. Its reading will begin our search for answers to the above questions regarding high fuel prices.

THE ARTICLE: "CONGRESS HUSTLES AMERICA"

Have you been hustled lately? Well, you may have if you concur with the notion that Congress and the President are doing all that they can to immediately bring down high gas prices. Most Congressional members say they recognize the need for Congress to help bring down fuel prices, but then they outline ideas, sometimes worthwhile, to bring down fuel prices "not now", but in the years ahead.

This approach represents the modus operandi of most members of Congress in recent years regarding gas prices: substantially ignore an obvious way that might bring down the price of gasoline immediately, because to do so requires confronting a very powerful and very, very <u>generous</u> group of individuals; namely, investment bankers and brokers in the financial services sector.

In order to camouflage their lack of courage and determination for such confrontation, many Democrats and Republicans in Congress have over the years instead focused on the correctness of drilling for oil in new locations. Or, they debate the correctness of investing more federal dollars to subsidize alternative energy sources.

In actuality, Congress could almost certainly bring down the price of fuel <u>immediately</u> and dramatically, if its members seriously challenged investment bankers and brokers who are speculating in the crude oil futures or swaps markets. These markets substantially determine the daily worldwide price of crude oil, which then quickly impacts fuel prices worldwide. Higher crude oil futures prices virtually always lead to higher gas prices.

Until early this century, the vast majority of participants in the "crude oil futures market" were so called "commercial buyers" and "commercial sellers". For example, commercial buyers might purchase futures contracts for companies like refineries or an airline company. They stand ready to actually receive delivery of crude oil.

Bowing to pressure from "big time" political donors in the financial sector, Congress, amazingly enough, in December of 2000, passed legislation which made it easier and "safer" for speculators to buy and sell crude oil futures type contracts. Now speculators (that is "betters") far outnumber traditional commercial buyers and commercial sellers of such contracts

Speculators in this sense include investment bankers, hedge fund managers, private equity fund managers, pension fund managers and frequently wealthy active investors. Speculators differ from traditional "commercial buyers" and "commercial sellers" of crude oil futures contracts, in that they typically never actually have crude oil to deliver nor do speculators typically actually plan to receive delivery of crude oil. Rather speculators, for example, buy crude oil futures contracts at current prices and hope that crude oil prices increase in the days ahead, allowing them to sell their contracts at a profit. Again, speculators are "betters", betting simply on whether the future price of crude oil will rise or fall.

If the number of speculators buying and selling crude oil contracts were, day in and day out, roughly equal, then potentially their impact on the price of crude oil might be less significant. So called experts disagree, but many feel that the run up in crude oil prices in recent years was not the result of a true shortage of crude oil supplies but rather the result of speculative buyers overwhelming the number of sellers. This creates what I describe as an "artificial" <u>increase</u> <u>in</u> <u>demand</u> for crude oil contracts, which can potentially drive up and keep up the price of crude oil (leading to higher gas prices).

Similarly, such speculators can create artificial increases in crude oil prices because they confuse; that is, "screw up" the daily "free market" process of establishing a <u>realistic</u> price for crude oil. Frequently the bets of these speculators focus more on "anticipated bets" of other fellow speculators, rather than focus on actual "real-life" supply and demand circumstances.

These "betting" speculators are eagerly looking for any remote rumor or other factoid that suggests crude oil may soon be in short supply. Frequently, they then subsequently bet that crude oil prices will rise. (Remember, during this century, betting speculators far outnumber true commercial participants in the crude oil markets…thanks to the legislative gift presented to investment bankers and brokers by a benevolent Congress and Bill Clinton in December of 2000, known as the Commodity Futures Modernization Act.)

The mere possibility that these speculators have forced Americans to pay perhaps three times as much for gas during the past ten years surely demands that Congress "do something".

To date, Congress has only considered ways to limit or better regulate such speculation. However, "better regulating" speculation is expensive, takes time and produces difficult to monitor grey areas that speculators will take advantage of. In addition, the debate over the potential negative impact of "betters" in the crude oil markets could go on forever (while the price of gas, conveniently enough, remains high).

My suggestion is for Congress to forget "better regulating", and instead, impose a complete ban (at least temporarily) of all American speculation in the crude oil markets… period. In other words, pass legislation that recreates the environment that was present in the crude oil markets during the 1980's and 1990's…and also during most of the long history of crude oil production. Then sit back and see what happens to the price of crude oil. (The ban, of course, would not affect traditional "commercial buyers" and "commercial sellers" of crude oil, provided they are willing to make or accept delivery of crude oil).

The upside potential of such Congressional action is huge. The price of crude oil during the next several months (if indeed speculators are the problem) could conceivably fall to as low as $25 per barrel as nervous speculators in mass liquidate at least part of their crude oil contracts, realizing that the "free flow of speculating dollars" into the crude oil markets could be seriously at risk. (A dramatic increase in the number of sellers relative to the number of buyers virtually always results in falling prices. In this case, a dramatic increase in sellers of crude oil contracts, could produce falling prices for crude oil, which in time would produce lower gasoline prices.)

On the other hand, the downside potential of the ban (if, in the unlikely event, crude oil prices do not fall) is that American commodity exchanges and "swaps" dealers <u>might</u> <u>temporarily</u> lose some speculative crude oil business to foreign exchanges.

Economically speaking, millions of Americans are in unprecedented trouble. An immediate, dramatic and ongoing drop in American fuel prices is perhaps the one single event that could begin the slow turnaround of the economic fortunes of millions of working middle class American families and small businesses.

So, to Congress I say, "Vote on proposals if necessary for offshore drilling and subsidizing alternative energy sources in the days ahead. But first, debate and vote on legislation <u>banning</u> American speculators from the crude oil futures market."

THE ARTICLE'S SIGNIFICANCE...
FOUR YEARS AGO AND NOW

Hopefully, you will agree that this article is as relevant in December of 2013 as it was over five years ago. The article identifies most (but not all) of the key players and institutions that I personally feel are responsible, either directly or indirectly, for years of artificially higher and unstable gas prices. Unless we or someone else intervene, these individuals will directly cause or at least allow, artificially high gas prices to continue for many years.

In addition, the article outlines a unique and rarely if ever discussed solution to the problem; that is, "a complete ban on crude oil speculation". Understanding "this solution" requires that you the reader clearly recognize the difference in traditional "commercial buyers" and "commercial sellers" on the one hand, and straight-up betters (referred to as speculators) on the other. It is these betters, I argue, that should be banned, because they can cause increases in retail prices for end line consumers (by creating "artificial increases in demand"). Again, regarding virtually any product (where the supply is constant), an increase in demand for that product, whether the increase is real or artificial, will create higher prices for consumers, whether it be at the gas pump, the grocery store or the local mall.

THE CRUDE OIL FUTURES MARKET...
FOCUSING ON WHAT IS IMPORTANT

Before moving to the next chapter, I should better discuss the so called crude oil futures market. Throughout this book I will refer to this market and the negative economic impact on middle income Americans of Congressional action in December of 2000, which effectively encouraged more "betters" to enter the crude oil markets.

So what is the crude oil futures market? It is, simply put, a vast market that allows commercial buyers, commercial sellers and (more recently) "betters" to enter contracts to buy or sell a specified quantity of crude oil at a specific price for future delivery on a specific date (thus the name, "futures" market). The worldwide price of crude oil varies from day to day and different grades of crude oil have different prices.

For example, the daily price per barrel of West Texas Intermediate oil (WTI), Brent crude oil (on a London Exchange) and crude oil from various Middle Eastern countries are frequently quoted…and their prices per barrel frequently differ. Per barrel prices in the so called "physical crude oil market" may also vary. (In this book, when I quote a specific price for a barrel of crude oil, I am typically referring to the per barrel price of West Texas Intermediate oil.)

Crude oil futures contracts are sometimes sold, resold, "cancelled out", etc. Both "betters" and commercial participants buy and sell such contracts. The crude oil futures market typically helps establish the "spot market price" for crude oil, which is the price required for immediate delivery of crude oil.

Crude oil is sold as a commodity. Thus, contracts for its purchase and sale are traded at commodity exchanges worldwide. The Crude Oil Mercantile Exchange is a physically present commodities exchange in New York where crude oil contracts are traded. Traders at such exchanges, of course, have to follow the rules and regulations established by the Exchange and are subject to regulation by the Commodities Futures Trading Commission of the Federal government.

DANGEROUS HOMBRES: OVER THE COUNTER CRUDE OIL SWAPS CONTRACTS

The crude oil "futures" market also includes a vast, highly opaque, and much less regulated market sometimes referred to as the "over-the-counter market". This market allows individuals (and companies) to enter private, customized contracts that in effect, "bet" on the future price of crude oil using, for example, over-the-counter swaps contracts, etc.

So, very broadly speaking, two distinct ways exist for using "future delivery" type contracts to bet on crude oil price fluctuations. The first would be the classic, true blue crude oil futures contracts traded on regulated exchanges. The second way would be the highly unregulated, hugely popular, computerized, over the counter "swaps-type" contracts.

It is interesting that one of the several ways that the Commodity Futures Modernization Act, passed in December of 2000, promoted increased crude oil speculation is this. The legislation made clear that "over the counter swaps type derivatives" were not, in fact, "true blue" crude oil futures contracts. For years, "betters" that were using "unregulated" swaps contracts worried about the outside chance that a U.S. Court might, for example, rule that "swaps contracts" really, really were "futures contracts" after all.

Since most buyers and sellers of such "swaps contracts" are not typically following the rules and regulations imposed on "true blue crude oil futures contracts" sold at regulated exchanges, the Court's ruling could in effect, mean that such "swaps contracts" were now unenforceable. Thus, potentially trillions (with a "t") of dollars of swaps contracts could be affected. A shrewd, heady, sophisticated, very wealthy investment banker might then be unable to collect on a hugely successful bet that he had placed over a month ago on the direction of crude oil prices.

In this book when I refer to crude oil futures contracts or the crude oil futures market, my intent is to include both types of contracts (discussed above) for purchasing or "betting" on the direction of crude oil prices. In addition, every argument that I make against crude oil speculation, also applies to speculation in the "gasoline futures market". For example, when I argue for a complete ban on speculation in the "crude oil futures market", I am also arguing for a complete ban on speculation in the "gasoline futures market".

WHAT ABOUT…THE "GASOLINE" FUTURES MARKET?

The gasoline futures market in America is much smaller and much less publicized than the vast worldwide crude oil futures market. Over the years, gasoline futures prices typically increase when the price of crude oil futures rise, and they fall when crude oil futures decline. (After all, the largest cost by far when producing gasoline is the cost of the raw material, which is crude oil).

31

During the last few weeks of January, and all of February 2013, gasoline futures prices rose significantly, while crude oil futures prices remained relatively stable. The price of regular gasoline in the metro Atlanta area during the same time period rose from roughly $3.15, up to $3.80 per gallon.

This two month, largely unexplained, very unusual if not historic, divergence of gasoline futures prices from crude oil futures prices simply makes it clear that "betters" in the gasoline futures market need to be "completely banned" just as I have suggested that "betters" in the crude oil futures market be "completely banned"

MAKING THE COMPLICATED...
A LITTLE LESS COMPLICATED

As you might expect, buying, selling or betting on crude oil prices can be complicated and confusing. I am not an expert, but I understand the process reasonably well. However, I do not see any real advantage in discussing in detail such subjects, terms or phrases as follows: forward contracts, sophisticated parties, counterparties, long positions, short positions, put options, call options, index funds, exchange traded funds, mark to market, individualized negotiation, swap futures contracts, etc. Rather, understanding the rules involved or the precise ways that crude oil is traded, is less important than clearly understanding the difference in traditional "commercial" traders versus traders that are simply "betters". Consider the following example.

You the reader likely do not have one thousand barrels of crude oil to ship, nor are you looking to actually receive one thousand barrels of crude oil. Thus, you are not a potential "commercial" trader of crude oil. However, if you have the money (quite a bit of money) and you wake up tomorrow with the notion that crude oil is absolutely going to significantly rise in price during the next few weeks, you could subsequently place a large bet on that notion. Unfortunately, you would not call Las Vegas to place such a bet. If you could and did, then the rest of us would not care whether your bet was a winner or loser. We would not be personally economically affected as a result of your bet.

Instead of calling Las Vegas you would, unfortunately, most likely place such a bet with your favorite investment banker or stock broker who has access to the crude oil futures market, commodity index funds, etc. He would likely purchase crude oil futures contracts or use "commodity swaps" that in effect would allow you to bet that crude oil prices will rise. You would thus become a "better"; that is, a "speculator" regarding the future price of crude oil. (You would not be required to make delivery or accept delivery of crude oil). Now your bet becomes very relevant to me and tens of millions of other Americans as well as individuals around the world. Your bet, combined with thousands of other bets, that crude oil prices will rise, might potentially actually "help" the ever changing price of crude oil to rise in the days ahead (resulting in higher gas prices).

CHAPTER TWO

INCREASING RETAIL PRICES:
ILLUSTRATING THE ROLE OF BETTERS

After reading the previous chapter, you likely understand the potential dangers of "runaway" betting in any commodities market, particularly the crude oil futures market. Such "speculation" can create "artificial increases in demand" in a market. As mentioned frequently, "real" or "artificial" increases in demand (relative to supply) almost always result in <u>higher</u> prices for end-line retail products. To better illustrate the significance of such "artificial increases in demand" and to better clarify the negative implications of "betters" in the crude oil futures market, consider the following example of the "peace lily market" with and without "betting" speculators.

BUYING PEACE LILIES...
IN THE REAL WORLD

During the 32 years that my wife and I owned retail stores we sold many different items. However, during the entire period we always sold live indoor tropical plants. Our stores had a "hard earned" reputation for selling indoor plants at "great prices".

There was, of course, no actual "commodities market" for various indoor plants. Thus, I, as a "commercial buyer" had to personally negotiate prices with nursery owners who were growing indoor plants. They would be the "commercial sellers" (the crude oil futures market before 2001 was dominated similarly by commercial buyers and commercial sellers as described earlier).

The competitive nature of our retail stores demanded that we obtain indoor plants for resale at the very lowest wholesale price possible. Thus, in the earlier years of our business, I hooked a 24-foot cargo trailer to a 318 Dodge Van and drove to Apopka, Del Ray Beach or Goulds, Florida. There I would personally, face to face, negotiate with indoor plant nursery owners regarding wholesale plant prices (in later years such negotiations took place over the phone). Interestingly, the "official" printed price list of tropical plants at a particular plant nursery, was frequently irrelevant.

The plant nursery owner considered many factors in deciding how cheaply he could sell me the indoor plants. Among them were (1) how regularly was I going to visit his nursery to buy plants, (2) did he have an excess amount of certain plants, (3) how much of a supply of plants did other local competing nurseries have on hand, (4) how many plants would he need for his other wholesale customers and (5) the plant buying season involved.

In the end, the commercial nursery owner got the best price he thought that he could receive at the time. I, as a commercial buyer, negotiated and typically received the best prices (and best values) that I could logically hope to receive. This, in turn, allowed me to eventually return to Atlanta and sell the (handpicked) assorted indoor plants at a very competitive price. In the end, our retail customers benefitted economically. They were able to purchase high quality indoor tropical plants and frequently save money at the same time.

This personal experience of buying indoor plants is a process that is similarly completed by business owners throughout America and the world millions of times each day. It is called free market capitalism and is based upon simple "supply and demand economics". As I will repeat often, not philosophically, but as someone who has "lived it", true free market capitalism is a beautiful thing, because it fairly rewards competitive entrepreneurs (and hopefully employees), while simultaneously promoting low prices and good value for retail customers. The process has been occurring naturally for thousands of years with frequently little need of government interference or regulation.

Two factors are absolutely essential to guarantee that free market capitalism eventually maximizes savings for end line retail customers. First, a commercial seller and commercial buyer must be able to accurately gauge the current and future supply of and demand for a given product. The second factor is an adequate amount of true competition throughout the process. In other words, the competitive forces of "real" supply and demand must rule the day.

These two very important factors were virtually always present during the 32 years that I purchased indoor plants for resale. I, as a commercial buyer, never had to worry about artificially high wholesale plant prices resulting from "artificial" increases in demand created by "betting speculators." However, to illustrate the potential economic dangers of such speculators, consider two different scenarios regarding supply and demand in the "indoor plant market".

SUPPLY AND DEMAND ECONOMICS...
IN MOTION

When buying indoor plants from Florida, I and most other "commercial buyers", understood that the prices we would have to pay for plants varied based on the season. During the spring and early summer, I might have to pay $9.50 for a "pretty average" peace lily grown in an 8-inch pot. (This plant is a staple for most indoor plant retailers and florists, because the plant is frequently purchased for funerals.)

However, if I drove to Apopka, Florida during the hot summer months, I was always able to purchase from a commercial nursery owner, peace lilies potted in 8-inch pots for maybe only $6.50 (instead of $9.50). In addition, these peace lilies purchased in the summer would have up to 40% more foliage and blooms than the ones purchased in the spring.

So over the years when I purchased peace lilies in July, I would expect to get more plant for less money compared to the peace lilies that I had purchased a few months earlier in March. The reason for the price difference was a reflection of supply and demand economics. In the spring or early summer, the demand for indoor tropical plants at retail plant stores, nurseries, grocery stores, chain stores and other plant retailers is very high. Commercial buyers from thousands of retail plant outlets, east of the Mississippi River, purchase large quantities of indoor tropical plants from Florida. During this time period, nurserymen in Florida frequently have trouble growing enough peace lilies (for example) to satisfy this dramatically increased demand. Thus, they typically raise their prices on 8" potted peace lilies in response to the "true" increases in demand.

As the months go by, peace lilies grown in 8-inch pots continue to grow in wholesale plant nurseries in various parts of Florida. By June or July, however, the number of such plants being ordered by retail outlets begins to decline sharply, so the supply of peace lilies available increases and the "true" demand for such plants decreases. Thus, not surprisingly, the wholesale price of peace lilies declines. Nurserymen, growers, and brokers of peace lilies are forced to sharply reduce the price of their product, as commercial buyers from retail outlets competitively search for the best prices available on peace lilies.

Since I and other commercial buyers for retail outlets would now be paying considerably less for peace lilies, then retail customers would also pay less. (For simplicity, I have focused on the price of peace lilies planted in 8 inch pots. In reality when I purchased indoor plants from Florida, I purchased many different varieties planted in six or eight different size containers. Virtually all of these plants followed the pattern of the peace lilies regarding seasonal price fluctuations. Thus, any reader seeking to maximize value and perhaps save money when buying retail indoor plants, should make their purchase during the summer, fall or winter months).

EXCESS PROFITS FOR JOHN THE NURSERYMAN...SPECULATORS OVERWHELM APOPKA, FLORIDA

So, during the 32 years that I purchased indoor plants from Florida, competition driven, true free market capitalism was on display. However, what happens if speculators (that is betters) are allowed into the picture? To further illustrate the potential dangers of such speculation, consider the following hypothetical example of speculation in the market for indoor tropical plants.

I "hook up" my trailer and drive 460 miles to Apopka, Florida in July to purchase indoor plants. My first stop is at a long time personal supplier who specializes in growing peace lilies. I need about 30 peace lilies grown in 8-inch pots. I am expecting that John, the nursery owner and I will eventually agree to a price of $6.50 to $7.00 per plant.

I suppose I could have gotten together with John, say back in February or March, and we could have written and signed a contract (similar to a "forward contract"), whereby I would know exactly what I would have to pay John for 8-inch peace lilies on today's visit. However, during the previous 50 or so plant buying visits to Florida, I very rarely had trouble finding good quality 8-inch peace lilies somewhere. Plus, since

I was investing time and money to drive from Atlanta to Florida, I wanted to personally see the plants that I would be buying, before deciding how much I would pay for them.

The point to be made here is this. Signing contracts for future delivery at specified prices is not a problem as long as the participants in the signings are "real" commercial buyers and commercial sellers. That process has been going on for many, many years in the commodities markets. The problem of potential "artificial increases in demand" being created, only occurs when betters and speculators (not commercial buyers or sellers) sign such contracts for future delivery.

So I arrive at John's nursery and ask him what kind of deal he can give me on 30 peace lilies potted in 8-inch containers. Though John has a greenhouse full of "very nice" peace lilies, he tells me that he actually has relatively few peace lilies to sell. He continues by saying that he could probably sell me 30 of the 8-inch peace lilies, but they would cost me $22 per plant.

My response would be, "you are kidding?" His reply is that many of the peace lilies are sold for "future delivery". I would reply "I don't understand. No commercial buyer is going to pay a wholesale price of $22 for an 8-inch peace lily, FOB Florida. Who is buying these plants at that price? These 8-inch peace lilies are very nice, but still I could not take them back to Atlanta to sell. I would be lucky to sell these peace lilies for $19 to our retail customers."

John's response might be, "Bob, I am sorry. I actually do not exactly know who is buying the plants. Something about Congress passed a law that makes it easier for Wall Street Bankers to speculate. These guys have been driving around town the last few weeks in big Mercedes Benz cars, and I mean the fancy ones, buying up a bunch of indoor plants from the nurseries around here. They pay us these crazy prices for our plants and we are supposed to hold them for future delivery. At first they only paid me $13 for my peace lilies, but then a different fellow came in last week. He gave me $22 per plant. Are you believing that?"

John might continue, "Bob you have been a loyal customer and long-time friend. I wish I could sell you some peace lilies for six or seven dollars, but I think I better wait to see if some more Mercedes Benz pull up in front of my nursery. Maybe the next guy will offer me $30.00 per peace lily. I haven't told you before, but I am having a really hard time lately making the monthly mortgage payments on this nursery."

My response to John would likely be no response, just stunned silence. I could see myself walking over to the vending machine in John's office, buying and instantly consuming a can of diet coke (it is 94 degrees with a humidity of 65% both inside and outside of John's office). Eventually, I would genuinely congratulate John on the fact that he was able to make excess profits on the crude oil that he produced....excuse me, tons of excess profit on the 8-inch peace lilies that he had grown.

I would leave John's nursery and spend the rest of the day sweating and looking around Apopka for the plants I needed. In the end, I might be forced to drive back to Atlanta with a substantially empty 24-foot trailer in tow.

This hypothetical experience of purchasing indoor plants is an attempt to show the potential negative impact (and confusion) that occurs when "non-commercial buyers" (that would be "betters") compete with each other and also compete with actual "commercial buyers" (that would be me) to purchase a product. The potential negative impact is the creation of "artificial increases in demand," which in turn can create artificially high prices, whether it be $22 peace lilies or $120 per barrel crude oil (leading to $4.00 per gallon gas).

In reality, for many reasons, you will never find any hedge fund managers, stock brokers or other investment bankers walking through the greenhouses in Apopka, Florida, buying 8-inch peace lilies and then speculating on future potential price increases. One reason for their absence is that indoor tropical plants are not a necessity. Thus, no guarantee exists that "real commercial buyers" (like myself) will continue to buy peace lilies, if the wholesale price is artificially inflated by speculation. In the hypothetical example above, I refuse to buy peace lilies at the inflated price. Virtually every other commercial buyer will refuse to pay $22 for peace lilies. In the end, these hypothetical investment bankers and other speculators would "be stuck" with tens of thousands of peace lilies to deal with.

COMMODITIES MARKET FOR NECESSITIES:
WHERE SPECULATORS TAKE ROOT

Not so however in the case of crude oil. Crude oil is a necessity because gasoline and other fuel are necessities. Thus, big time betters and stock brokers know that "commercial buyers", as well as other "betters", will continue to buy crude oil contracts, even though the asking price for such crude oil is potentially artificially high as a result of the "artificial increases in demand" created by speculators.

So many of the commodities markets in which speculators particularly enjoy betting, involve commodities that are absolute necessities or are close to it. However, a few commodity markets are popular with speculators even though the commodity in question is not a necessity. The commodities markets for precious metals are a good example.

The commodity "gold" for instance, is not a necessity for most of the world's population. However, the actual demand for gold is relatively high among more prosperous and wealthier individuals, particularly during the last 10 years.

No one knows for sure, from a historical perspective, exactly what a reasonable price for an ounce of gold really is. This fact, plus the fact that a large number of "commercial participants" are continually entering and leaving the market, makes speculation in gold very popular with investment bankers, brokers and other active investors.

During most of the 1980's and all of the 1990's, gold averaged around $300 per ounce. In early 2002, gold sold for $316 an ounce. Until this century, dramatic increases in the price of gold most frequently occurred in response to anticipated or actual "inflationary pressure on prices". During the last ten years, inflation has easily averaged less than 3% per year in America, yet in October of 2012 gold sold for almost $1800 per ounce. (In recent months, the price of gold has declined dramatically, currently selling for less than $1,400 per ounce). Two months from now no one knows what an ounce of gold will be selling for. The significant fact is this. Most of the world's inhabitants do not care.

In other words, when "artificial increases in demand" creep into the crude oil futures market and potentially create higher crude oil prices, then thousands of millions of middle class small business owners and billions of individuals around the world suffer economically as fuel prices rise. When the price of commodities like gold and platinum rise to historic levels, potentially because of "artificial increases in demand", the vast majority of the world's population is unaffected.

So common sense would seem to dictate that the Federal government of the United States and the governments of industrialized countries worldwide, would seriously and very publicly debate the potential negative impact of speculation in various commodity markets, where "absolute necessities" are traded (including the crude oil markets). However, do not look for any major public discussions, let alone significant changes in the current status quo. Speculation in commodity markets is frequently a very lucrative business for the financial services sector, and as I will note often, the financial services sector is politically very well connected and is very generous in its financial contributions to candidates of both political parties.

The bottom line is this. Once the congressional legislation in December of 2000 allowed speculators to overwhelm the crude oil markets, the market in my opinion simply no longer remains relevant in establishing an accurate daily price for crude oil. "It's not even close." True market driven forces of supply and demand are overwhelmed by the sheer volume of "daily bets" by speculators.

My oft repeated contention is that such daily "ten million dollar type bets" not only interfere with establishing the true value of a barrel of crude oil, but the bets also have a tendency to inflate the actual price of a barrel of crude oil. For example, it is my opinion that "betters", frequently in unison, "deliberately over-react to the slightest hint or rumor of potential current or future shortages of crude oil, and then quickly "buy" crude oil futures type contracts…a way of betting that crude oil prices will rise and also a way of potentially helping to cause increases in the ever-changing price of crude oil.

On the other hand, especially in the absence of such betters, experienced, long time "commercial buyers" of crude oil (like experienced commercial buyers of peace lilies) would likely take a "wait and see" attitude towards such "rumors" of future crude oil shortages. Twenty years of $15 to $25 dollar per barrel crude oil during the

1980's and 1990's is explained by this "wait and see approach" of veteran commercial buyers of crude oil...as well as the substantial absence of crude oil speculators during the 1980's and 1990's.

In comparison, the past ten years of this century have seen record high crude oil prices even though a monarch from a crude oil producing country and a CEO of a large international oil company tell us (what even a casual observer recognizes), that there has been no real shortage of crude oil during the past ten years.

A TON OF RICE: WHAT IS IT WORTH?

This book focuses on the negative impact of speculators in the crude oil markets. However, before moving to the next chapter and at my daughter's suggestion, I would like to offer a quick illustration of the potential negative impact of commodity markets' speculators on the price of food staples. Consider, for example, the commodity "rice"...the primary food staple for well over half of the world's population.

Vast amounts of rice are grown worldwide each year. Much of the rice is not sold per se on commodities exchanges. Governments of some countries discourage the exportation of rice, in order to insure that its own citizens have an ample supply. The governments of various countries subsidize rice farmers; that is, they sometimes pay the farmers more than the "going" market price for rice. These governments then sometimes store their rice purchases until the going price of rice increases, etc.

Nevertheless, huge quantities of rice are exported by various countries and are frequently traded on commodity exchanges or via swaps contracts. Thus, the price established for rice using futures type contracts/bets, frequently affects the price of rice that is not actually traded on commodity exchanges.

This book does not include graphs. However, the internet has plenty of graphs available that track the price of a metric ton of rice (and, of course, many other commodities) over a specific number of months or years. Very roughly speaking, in the commodities market, rice cost $150 to $350 per metric ton, during the years 1983 until 2007.

However, during the year 2007, the price of rice began to rapidly increase, eventually reaching almost $1,000 per metric ton. The price of a metric ton of rice had almost tripled. Several individuals of Chinese descent, with whom we did business, were buying and stockpiling 100 pound bags of rice in the latter months of 2007. They were truly afraid that the price of rice might continue to rise to a point that they could no longer afford to purchase the product.

It is important to remember that in most industrialized countries, citizens on average spend less than 20% of their yearly income on food purchases. In underdeveloped countries, the percentage spent on food purchases by families may approach 80% of yearly income. One can only imagine the chaos, anger, confusion and fear of such individuals during the year 2007, as the price of many long time food staples began rapidly increasing.

Then during 2008, the price of rice rapidly declined from roughly $1,000 per metric ton to around $500 per metric ton Also, beginning in July 2008, crude oil prices fell (temporarily) from a $147 per barrel down to $32 per barrel in less than one year.

For me, without question, only one explanation accounts for such rapid increases and declines in the price of rice (as well as most other commodities). The explanation is that traders, betters, and speculators (or whatever you want to call them) bid up the price of rice to ridiculously high prices using massive amounts of credit to create "artificial increases in demand".

When the hugely inflated financial and commodities markets bubble began to rapidly deflate in 2007 and especially in 2008, the availability of credit began to disappear.   Thus, speculators and "betters" were frequently forced to sell most of their futures contracts to cover margin calls, etc. In other words, the previous "artificial increases in demand" disappeared and the price of rice and most other commodities fell "like a rock", as the number of commodity "sellers" vastly outnumbered the number of commodity "buyers".

So the price of rice fell during 2008 by almost 100%. The worldwide actual consumption of rice during the same time period likely fell less than 4%. (Ditto…the crude oil markets. The price of crude oil fell 600% in less than one year. The actual consumption of crude oil, gasoline and other fuels during this time period probably fell by less than 10%.) Obviously, these rapid price declines in such commodity prices cannot be explained by capitalistic principles of supply and demand economics. That is, these historic declines in price did not result from vast increases of production or massive decreases in consumption. Rather, only "rabid betting" by speculators can explain this phenom.

Interestingly, during the time frame in question, around the years 2007 and 2008, the wholesale or retail prices of peace lilies potted in 8-inch containers did not increase or decline by 100% (or even 10%). Ditto the price of greeting cards, name brand tennis shoes, new/used automobiles, doctor visits, etc.

So, again, and again, and again, the only logical explanation for the rapid price increases and the rapid price declines during 2007 and 2008 of rice (as well as crude oil and other commodities), is that a relatively small group of investment bankers, stockbrokers, hedge fund managers, equity fund managers and "active" wealthy investors, etc. frequently made fortunes betting (and promoting) price fluctuations in the various commodity markets, while billions of the world's population suffered. Still, even today, these "betters" continue, in my opinion, to frequently overwhelm the commodities markets involving rice, crude oil and other essentials, sometimes causing price instability or actually driving up prices for end line consumers.

The questions are…how long will the world's population tolerate such anti-capitalistic betting? How long will the world's politicians and members of the world's media outlets essentially understand what happened (as described) in the food commodities markets back in 2007 and 2008, but ask few questions and demand no answers? Or asked differently, how long will so many allow so few to create so much... economic hardship?

CHAPTER THREE

TOWARD GAS AT $1.25: THE PLAN

So having at least a rough idea of how the crude oil futures market typically works is important. Using a little common sense to recognize the potential danger to your wallet of "artificial increases in demand" within the crude oil futures market (or any market) is equally important. However, to understand how my plan to promote $1.25 per gallon gas differs from other proposed solutions, I need to explain several key notions relating to the "Congress Hustles America" article, presented in Chapter One.

THE NOTION OF…"ABSOLUTE PROOF"

Despite the instability and generally higher crude oil and gas prices that have occurred this century after "big time" investors were allowed to greater speculate in the crude oil futures market, investment bankers, brokers and their many, many, many defenders will claim that no "absolute proof" exists that speculators are causing higher and less stable crude oil prices. They argue that speculators add "liquidity" to the crude oil markets. They "grease the cogs". They make "hedging" easier within the market, etc. etc. If crude oil futures prices rose to $300 per barrel, then these so called experts, speculators and many Congressional members would still smile and claim…"no absolute proof exists".

For me, the primary goals of "competition driven free market capitalism" are (1) to fairly reward successful competitive business owners and employees; and (2) promote the best values (and prices) that are possible on an ever increasing, wide range of products for "end line" retail customers. In this regard, the presence of speculators, in virtually any market, can potentially interfere with these two goals (as the earlier example of "the peace lily market" illustrated).

The fact that some commercial participants in a market (particularly producers) claim that the presence of speculators "adds liquidity" or is somehow "convenient" is irrelevant and anti-capitalistic, if in fact such conveniences cause end line consumers to pay more for their products. As will be discussed later, you will not find many individuals who own multiple oil wells somewhere in West Texas (now receiving maybe five times more for a barrel of crude oil than they did during the 1990's) complaining about the presence of "speculation" in the crude oil futures market during the last ten years.

As discussed in the introduction and also in Chapter One, most politicians who could conceivably help end crude oil speculation, would typically prefer to "completely" ignore the subject of "speculation" in the crude oil markets. If forced to broach the subject, most politicians invoke some variant of the "absolute proof" argument. They may then suggest that perhaps "better regulation" of crude oil trading is needed, which would "supposedly" have to take place at the appropriate regulatory agency within the Federal government.

THE NOTION OF "BETTER REGULATION" VS THE NOTION OF "A COMPLETE BAN"

During the month of October 2008, I was talking to an editor of "The Hill" Newspaper, one of the two newspapers that cater to Congressional members and other federal employees. I had written a 450 word article similar to the one that I used in the first chapter of this book. I was asking him to consider publishing the article. During the course of our conversation, he said in effect that my description of the potential dangers of speculation in the crude oil market was not exactly a unique observation. He noted that many individuals had already figured that out.

I then clarified to him that my explanation of "how" crude oil speculation was potentially creating high fuel prices was necessary but not the focus of my article. My article, I argued, was important because I discussed a unique way to deal with crude oil speculation; that is, simply ban the practice. I argued that virtually all other publicly proposed solutions suggested "better regulating", not banning the practice.

The U.S. Commodity Futures Trading Commission was (and is) usually assigned "to better regulate" speculation. My proposal was to bypass this federal agency and instead, challenge Americans to petition Congress to personally ban speculation; that is take away the very right to speculate (at least temporarily). If the temporary ban on speculation was successful and resulted in dramatically lower crude oil prices (followed by dramatically lowered gas prices), then presumably Congress would make the ban permanent. (The short article was eventually posted on "The Hill" website).

To date Congress has completely ignored the concept of a "complete ban" (even a temporary one). Instead Congress (when "pressured") has during the last ten years only considered ways to limit or "better regulate" crude oil speculation. However, as noted earlier, "better regulating" speculation is expensive, takes time and produces difficult to monitor grey areas that speculators will likely take advantage of.

THE COMMODITY FUTURES TRADING COMMISSION: "PROVIDING COVER"

The typical scenario goes something like this…gas prices <u>really</u> rise but most Congressional members "look the other way". Eventually, however constituents begin to "seriously" complain, Congressional members feel the heat and eventually promise to have the Commodity Futures Trading Commission, an agency of the Federal Government, to "look into the situation" and determine if more regulation of speculators is needed.

The problem is that the Commodity Futures Trading Commission does not seem particularly effective in regulating crude oil speculation. At best, the Commodity Futures Trading Commission operates, that is regulates, in "slow motion". At worst the Agency, rather than regulating, seems possibly more adept at "providing cover" for investment bankers and wealthy active investors who are speculating on the future price of crude oil.

For example, in October of 2011, the Commodity Futures Trading Commission approved new rules designed to "better regulate" very large crude oil speculators. These rules were scheduled to take effect some time in 2012 or maybe 2013…no big rush. Some observers considered these new "tougher rules" to be weak and inadequate to deal with crude oil speculation.

Nevertheless, the two primary lobbying groups for investment bankers <u>successfully</u> challenged the new CFTC rules in court, with a ruling being handed down in October of 2012. For sure, "better regulation" will <u>not</u> provide the so called "absolute proof" that is apparently needed to force Congress or the President to act decisively against crude oil speculators.

Interestingly enough, President Obama last year, after a sharp ongoing spike in gasoline prices, made a number of speeches in which he called upon Congress to pass new legislation that would, you guessed it, "better regulate" the crude oil futures market. The notion of taking tougher action against speculators was almost certainly not even considered. Many of President Obama's closest advisors and friends are current or former high powered investment bankers and brokers.

So, it seems to me, that for well over ten years, "the threat" of better regulating crude oil speculation has in effect "protected such speculation." In other words, if the focus is on "better regulating", then the <u>actual</u> <u>right</u> (or the actual privilege) of being able to "bet" in the crude oil commodities market is either accepted or ignored. This book, of course, questions the legitimacy of the very right (promoted in December of 2000) to engage in such speculation.

THE CHALLENGE: WHAT TO DO?

My feeling is this, "enough is enough". If investment bankers and wealthy, politically powerful or otherwise strategically positioned defenders of crude oil speculation want so called "absolute proof", then you, I and millions of others should give it to them. We should demand, after adequate Congressional debate, that Congress immediately ban all speculation in the crude oil markets. (Notice I said "ban" not "better regulate").

The ban initially could last for three months and begin two weeks after passage of the needed legislation. (Traditional so called "commercial buyers" and "commercial sellers" of crude oil futures contracts would be allowed absolute free access into the crude oil markets, provided, of course, that they are willing to actually deliver or receive shipments of crude oil.)

Such a ban could be established in one of two ways. Congress could repeal specific parts of the legislation passed in 2000, called "The Commodity Futures Modernization Act" that allowed in effect, "betters" to more safely speculate in the crude oil markets. Alternatively, and preferably, Congress could simply vote to make it "criminally" illegal for individual Americans or American based companies to speculate in crude oil, using the crude oil futures market or any other financial instruments to do so.

Such dramatic action by Congress (a complete ban on crude oil speculation) is both practical and moral in nature. Crude oil speculation in its various forms is complicated, popular, and frequently very profitable. Defenders and detractors of the practice are not in short supply. The debate could go on for 100 years (while gas prices remain high). Only <u>one</u> path can establish absolute proof. That path requires a "complete ban" on such crude oil speculation and then "sit back" and see what happens to the price of crude oil in the days following the ban.

Actually, the implied notion that "absolute proof" is a requirement for tough Congressional action is nowhere written in stone. To me, the <u>mere</u> <u>possibility</u> that speculators have forced hundreds of millions of Americans and billions worldwide to pay perhaps three times more during the past 10 years than they should have for a gallon of gas, demands tough Congressional action. Many of the individuals sitting in Congress right now were among the Congressional members who voted in favor of the legislation passed in December of 2000, which eventually encouraged bankers and investors in mass to place bets simply on the future direction of crude oil prices. If portions of that legislation were a huge mistake, then it is past time for Congress to finally correct the problem.

GOVERMENT INTERFERENCE...IN THE AFFAIRS OF PRIVATE BUSINESSES

As a former longtime business owner, I am not generally a fan of government interference with the operation of private businesses. However, it is abundantly clear to me that the financial services sector used its incredible wealth and political influence, leading up to December of 2000, to encourage passage of the Commodity Futures Modernization Act. This legislative gift to "Wall Street" types, among many other things, greatly encouraged bankers to speculate in the crude oil futures market. They have since camped out there for the past 12 years.

I am not objecting in general to investors betting or speculating in the financial markets. That is the name of the game. In any given minute, hedge fund managers or private equity fund managers have millions of different ways they can bet their own or their client's money in financial markets all over the world.

However, common sense would seem to dictate that certain commodity markets should be "off limits" to our beloved hedge fund manager seeking to bet millions of dollars (most of it on credit) simply on whether the price of various commodities is headed "up" or "down". As described on previous pages, such betting interferes with naturally occurring "free market competition". Such betting creates instability and sometimes generally higher prices on commodities like crude oil, which then lead to higher fuel prices. This is exactly why speculation in various commodity markets was highly regulated or restricted in earlier years.

So, in effect, what the December of 2000 "legislative gift" promoted was huge amounts of extra profits for companies, executives, investors and employees associated with two of America's richest and most politically powerful business sectors; namely companies within the financial services sector and (as explained later) companies that produce crude oil. At the same time this "legislative gift" (that eventually led to higher gas prices, etc.) has proven to be an "economic hardship" for millions of middle class small business owners, as well as middle class families. Thus, in this particular case, "government intervention" is required to protect the economic interests of "weaker", less politically connected, businesses and families. In other words, Congress simply has to "take back" the wonderfully benevolent legislative gift that they provided to investment bankers in December of 2000.

If you agree that "enough is enough", then join me and possibly many others and petition your elected Congressional members to "ban" crude oil speculation. Each American has at least 4 elected representatives in Washington that should be contacted by phone, email or if possible, "in person." They include one member from the House of Representatives, 2 members from the Senate and the President.

At this point, for those readers who question their own ability to influence what goes on in Congress, please temporarily skip to Chapter 10, the last chapter of this book. This short chapter describes the problems and possibilities in confronting Congressional members.

CHAPTER FOUR

BANNING CRUDE OIL SPECULATION: IS IT REALLY POSSIBLE?

From personal experience, I can tell those of you who decide to join me in publicizing the potential negative role of speculation in the crude oil/gas futures market and also lobbying for a "complete ban" of such speculation, that you will face a variety of arguments against your efforts. However, the standard, perhaps most relevant argument that specifically deals with the notion of a "complete ban", goes something like this. "Bob, you don't understand. Completely banning speculation in the crude oil markets is impossible. Even if Congress passed legislation that immediately banned crude oil speculation in America or banned Americans from speculating in the crude oil markets anywhere else, then at the very least, multi-millionaire investors, hedge fund managers and private equity firm managers, would simply take their business to London, Hong Kong, Oman, etc. In other words, crude oil futures are bought and sold "over-the-counter" and traded through commodity and futures exchanges worldwide."

At first glance, this argument seems valid. Upon closer inspection this argument falls apart because it misses the point (not to mention the fact that crude oil speculation was substantially limited in America before the year 2000).

My proposal of a complete ban, at least temporarily, on Americans speculating in crude oil futures will result in one of several scenarios. Regardless of which scenario eventually unfolds, crude oil prices, and thus gas prices could eventually fall like a rock.

HOW ABOUT...
THE PERFECT SCENARIO

The first scenario unfolds along this line. A nobody, that would be me, writes a book that gets a little publicity. The book contains a plan, that if implemented could greatly restrict who is legally allowed to purchase crude oil futures contracts, crude oil commodity swaps, etc.

The plan requires that the citizenry of America call, email or otherwise communicate with their respective Washington politicians demanding that all Americans must be banned from "speculating" on crude oil prices. As the Congressional heat rises, Congressional members actually begin a real, very public debate on a "complete ban" of American crude oil speculation. As support for the "absolute ban" increases in Congress, the President would have no choice but to call the Presidents and Prime Ministers of other industrialized countries to see if they too would join America in banning crude oil speculation. The average everyday citizens of these industrialized countries, having already observed what

American citizens were doing, quite likely would similarly demand that their elected representatives put an end to crude oil speculation.

Eventually crude oil speculation would be made illegal throughout much of the industrialized world. Then for sure, the world's population could "sit back" and see what happens to the price of crude oil and gasoline. The possibility of "absolute proof" would truly be at hand.

HOW ABOUT...A "LESS THAN PERFECT" SCENARIO

However, this perfect scenario does not have to play out. Even if no other government, at least initially, joins America in attempting to ban crude oil (and gas) speculation, the dye still will have been cast, provided the potential economic problems of crude oil speculation and the notion of a "complete ban" have been highly publicized.

Investment bankers and brokers, holding perhaps millions of dollars of crude oil futures and swaps contracts, are counting on an unrestricted flow of dollars into the crude oil futures market (to keep prices high and provide for the purchase of their own crude oil futures and swaps contracts). Any serious potential threat to the free flow of speculators (and their cash) into the crude oil markets could quickly reduce the value of investment bankers' holdings. This prospect might encourage some such speculators to quickly sell part or all of their crude oil futures contracts. This potential abundance of sellers and shortage of buyers could eventually cause a down draft in the going price of crude oil futures contracts.

For sure, no self-respecting private equity fund manager wants to be the last investment banker to unload his investment in a speculative market that begins to have more sellers than buyers. Perhaps the worst fear of such big time investment bankers operating inside a potential speculative "bubble market" like the crude oil futures market, is to be the last banker reaching the exit door to sell his contracts, as the bubble bursts. (The only greater fear of such an investment banker is to actually trip, fall and be almost trampled to death by other investment bankers and brokers, including his brother-in-law, uncle, nephew and former college roommate, all trying to sell crude oil contracts as they rush toward the exit sign leaving the deflated crude oil "bubble market".)

"PUBLICITY": THE REAL KEY

A complete ban on speculation in the crude oil futures market imposed throughout the industrialized world, would add more permanence and stability to "lower crude oil and lower gas prices". Lower and more stable gas prices would of course be a huge benefit to business owners making various decisions throughout the industrialized world. In the absence of such a worldwide ban, widespread publicity and support for the "complete ban concept" should still guarantee substantial reductions in gas prices in the days ahead, as outlined above.

To answer skeptics of "a complete ban" on speculation in the crude oil market, such a worldwide ban is not necessarily needed (just preferred). What is absolutely needed is you, I and millions of others, publicizing the potential negative consequences of such speculation and a viable, quickly implemented plan to end it. Speculators in the crude oil markets will quickly get the message.

THE GOOD GUYS VERSUS THE BAD GUYS: A CLARIFICATION

Before going to the next chapter which begins Part 2 of the book, namely, "Oil Company Competition", a quick and final clarification regarding "speculation" is needed. During the previous four chapters, I have repeatedly made the distinction between so called commercial buyers and commercial sellers in the crude oil markets on the one hand, and speculators/betters on the other.

Further, I have described commercial buyers and commercial sellers as legitimate participants in the crude oil market, while "speculators" are illegitimate. In other words, commercial participants are the "capitalistic good guys", while speculators are the "anti-capitalistic bad guys".

Also, I (like many other commentators) have noted that one way to distinguish true blue commercial participants from speculators is that commercial participants, unlike betters, are willing to accept or make delivery of the commodity in question (like crude oil).

A key element of my plan to quickly bring down gas prices requires that "we the people" in effect force Congress to actually ban (or at least seriously threaten to ban) the "bad guys" from betting in the crude oil markets. Fortunately, for the vast majority of individuals participating in the crude oil markets, the criteria, "an ability to make or actually accept the physical delivery of crude oil", accurately distinguishes true commercial participants from speculators. In other words, we and Congress typically know who to ban and who not to ban from the crude oil markets.

However, it must be noted that a very small percentage of the total number of the world's crude oil "speculators" may also qualify as "commercial participants" in the crude oil markets, because they actually "really, really do" receive delivery of commodities like crude oil, and they eventually also sell and make delivery of the purchased crude oil or other commodity. In other words, these companies (including commercial and investment banks) purchase, warehouse, or otherwise store commodities like aluminum, copper, crude oil, etc. At the same time, these banks and other companies also speculate/bet, in separate company operations, on the future direction of the price of these various stored commodities. So again, these (relatively few) banks technically qualify as both speculators and commercial participants.

YES, "A REFERENCE"...
WHAT CAN I SAY?

A front page article in the July 27, 2013 edition of the Wall Street Journal written by Dan Fitzpatrick and

Christian Berthelsen, describes these "physical commodity type operations" by three of Wall Street's largest banks, in particular J.P. Morgan. The article was very informative and describes a business model that is not widely publicized. Its authors did not seem to take a particularly positive or negative position regarding "bankers as warehousemen". They did indicate that buying and storing physical commodities is currently less appealing to bankers than were such activities during the recent past.

OF GENERAL INTEREST: BEER DRINKERS BEWARE

Of general interest, the article points out that executives from some companies (for example, Miller Coors LLC), that are large users of various metals like aluminum, have complained that such "bank warehouses" are sometimes holding up aluminum shipments to their company and thereby increasing product cost. To me, it would seem that these "bank owned warehouses" could possibly be delaying such shipments of aluminum until the ever changing daily price of aluminum has reached "appropriate levels".

OF SPECIAL INTEREST: THREE DIFFERENT POINTS

As the author of this book, the Wall Street Journal article is relevant for at least three reasons. First, the article describes in some detail a clear <u>exception</u> to the general rule that is used to determine just who is actually a "speculator".

Secondly, the authors of the article note that some consumer advocates claim that banks used barges in which to store crude oil back in 2008, and thus helped force the price of crude oil to record highs of more than $140 per barrel,

Thirdly, the article describes several instances of special treatment by the Federal government regarding the financial services sector...a central complaint that I have expressed throughout this book. For example, the authors note that for decades banks were forbidden by the U.S. government to actually own commercial type assets like copper, aluminum, crude oil, etc. However, the article points out that U.S. Federal policy makers began deregulating bank operations in the 1990's. In particular, during this century, the Federal Reserve repeatedly granted large banks "special permission" to expand their operation and ownership of physical commodities.

STORING 175,000 TONS OF COPPER... "JUST BANKING AS USUAL"

With the blessing of the Federal Reserve, J.P. Morgan, as amazing as it seems, eventually came to own, according to the article, more than 70 facilities on four continents in order to purchase and store commercial metals. In December of 2010, J.P. Morgan reportedly had more than 175,000 tons of copper stored in its warehouses in London. More recently, by the end of March of 2013, the article notes that J.P. Morgan had leased almost 35 billion (with a "b") cubic feet of storage space for natural gas.

So during this century, Federal government regulators, Congress and the Federal Reserve have changed long standing rules and have allowed large commercial and investment banks to buy, store and potentially hoard large quantities of physical commodities like aluminum, copper and crude oil. Again, throughout this book, I have and will continue to describe such special treatment that investment bankers routinely receive from the Federal government.

BANNING SPECULATION: THE IMPACT OF "BARGE LEASING BANKERS"

However, the real point of this particular section of the chapter, and the very important question that must be answered is this. Does the fact that a relatively small number of speculators are "meeting the criteria" that allows them to qualify as "commercial participants", materially affect our plan to ban crude oil speculation and quickly bring down gas prices?

In other words, suppose that Congress decided to actually "ban crude oil speculation", but also decided that these large commercial/investment banks (as described above) could continue to buy, sell and bet in the crude oil markets. Would the continued presence of these bankers in the crude oil markets, who are buying and then storing crude oil in barges, materially impact our plan to quickly bring down gas prices? The answer is an emphatic "no".

First of all, as noted, the vast majority of speculators in the crude oil markets <u>do</u> <u>not</u> store crude oil in barges. Secondly, in the weeks ahead, Congress may (finally) take the logical course of action and restrict "speculating banks" from simultaneously buying, storing and betting on large amounts of physical commodities like aluminum and crude oil. Alternatively, such banks are reportedly seeking to sell or otherwise de-emphasize some of their "warehousing operations".

However, even if these "speculating, warehousing, barge leasing bankers" continue their current operations unabated, it does not matter. If we, as a group, convince Congress to seriously consider or actually ban crude oil speculation, then the battle (and the war) will have been won, as outlined in the previous section. Many tentative crude oil betters will begin leaving the market; that is, they will begin selling at least part of their crude oil futures contracts. Eventually, crude oil sellers will likely overwhelm crude oil buyers, and the price of crude oil (and gasoline) will fall dramatically.

A crude oil "better" may simply hold futures type contracts to purchase crude oil or "the better" may actually own millions of barrels of crude oil stored in a tanker (or crude oil pipelines). Either way, if the going price of crude oil, for example, falls 30% in one week, then these hypothetical participants (whether considered by Congress to be "betters" or "commercial participants") have a serious economic problem and decisions to deal with.

PART TWO

OIL COMPANY COMPETITION

CHAPTER FIVE

FORCING OIL COMPANIES TO COMPETE: THE SECOND STEP

Banning crude oil speculation is by far the most important step in bringing down the price of gasoline. However, to <u>maximize</u> the overall decline in fuel prices in the days ahead, a second step is required. This step involves forcing oil producing companies to more strongly compete with one another in a manner, for example, similar to the way that various airline companies frequently reduce airline fares to better compete with one another, day in and day out.

This lack of competition between oil producers has occurred primarily during the last 10 years, as crude oil futures prices have risen far above what it costs on average to bring a barrel of crude oil to the surface. On the other hand, during most of the 1980's and all of the 1990's, oil producing companies were indeed competing. As described, the crude oil futures price of a barrel of crude oil during this time period averaged around $15 to $25 per barrel, with the price of a barrel occasionally falling to a price as low as $8. Prices for regular gasoline averaged around 70 to 80 cents per gallon in the metro Atlanta area during this time frame.

During this roughly 20 year period, like much of the previous 100 plus years, investors were discouraged from speculating and potentially "bidding up" crude oil futures prices. As a result, oil producers, whether in Saudi Arabia or West Texas, had to accept "competition driven" low offers to purchase their crude oil. These offers were based on "the real", "the actual" supply and demand for crude oil (similar to my situation when buying tropical plants in Florida). These crude oil producers understood all too well that they had produced more crude oil than buyers actually needed, and at times were probably thankful to receive fifteen dollars for a barrel of crude oil. However, during this approximate 20 year period, no large international oil companies went out of business, but oil company executives and stockholders were probably a little bit fussy.

MIRACLES DO HAPPEN: ASK OIL COMPANY EXECUTIVES

But then a miracle of sorts occurred. As discussed earlier, Congress, in December of 2000, substantially completed the process, going on for years, of deregulating the financial markets, including the crude oil markets. Consequently, wealthy investment bankers and wealthy active investors could "more safely" and more aggressively "bet" in the crude oil markets. Within a few years the price of crude oil had doubled and then tripled, etc. Gas prices eventually rose to unprecedented highs.

So, here is a quick review. I have asserted through-out this book that crude oil speculators have forced crude oil prices during the last 10 years to rise to unrealistically high levels. This in turn has resulted in record high gas prices. For me, clearly crude oil speculators are the primary problem; the primary reason for 10 plus years of high gas prices.

However, I am now further asserting that during the past 10 plus years, large oil companies, had they been aggressively competing against one another, could have reduced this overall rise in fuel prices. In other words, once speculators drove up the price of a barrel of crude oil, gas prices were eventually bound to rise. However, as crude oil prices rose to artificially inflated highs, large oil companies have had ample opportunity, during the past 10 years, to at least partially reduce the various increases in gas prices…by aggressively competing with one another.

This lack of competition is not occurring at your local gas station pump. Profit margins for gas station owners and managers is, and has always been, typically very small. Rather, this lack of competition is occurring early on in the complex process of fuel production. It is occurring when oil producers in effect "sell" their crude oil to refineries, brokers, "themselves", etc.

Today, oil companies are obtaining crude oil from some of the same American oil wells and oil rigs from which they obtained crude oil during the 1980's and 1990's. As noted often, during that time period they were frequently receiving only $15 to $25 per barrel of crude oil.

Now, during recent years, such crude oil producers are frequently charging (and receiving) over $90 per barrel for crude oil sometimes originating from many of the exact same oil wells in service during the 1980's and 1990's. Profit margins have sometimes increased five-fold (from $15 per barrel, to $90 plus per barrel).

"GOOD GRIEF"…MORE ABOUT FREE MARKET CAPITALISM

Now consider my definition of free market capitalism based on 32 years as a small business owner: "In a truly capitalistic free-market environment, companies within a given industry are continuously seeking new products and new services to sell. Also, some companies are continuously seeking to sell existing, higher profit, established products at a cheaper price to the public than does the competition. Seeking to gain market share by cutting prices is virtually a given (in the absence of collusion) when "price point, competition-driven capitalism" is occurring. Always there seems to be someone down the mall or across the street who is willing to make less profit per sale, in order to increase overall sales and profits. Innovative and hard-working business owners and (hopefully) their employees benefit, and in the process, customers also benefit by receiving better value and lower prices."

It is true, of course, that virtually all businesses engage in competition at various levels. For example, most companies promote (and compete) regarding their customer service, their new products, their level of experience and expertise, their concern for the local community, etc. Oil companies can argue that they compete with each other regarding where and how much to spend on exploration for crude oil. However, in virtually all business sectors, "the bar of competition" is eventually raised and "price point competition" occurs naturally and continuously between businesses within a sector, and consumers, as described, benefit.

Occasionally, products or services are created or perfected by an individual or company to a degree that "price point competition" is less relevant or non-existent. Typically these products produced or services rendered are "particularly unique" or "in short supply". An example would be recent sales involving the IPhone and IPad. Another example would be a hair stylist, whose reputation is so esteemed that she charges a $150 for a hairstyling appointment, for which other hairstylists are charging only $10 to $20.

The important point here is that during the past 12 years, crude oil has not been in short supply. Neither is a barrel of crude oil particularly unique.

So, having read my personal definition of free market capitalism (with a focus on "price point competition"), what is missing in the above described selling of crude oil by large oil producers? The answer is, of course, there appears to be little or no "price point competition"; that is, there is no apparent attempt on the part of any major oil company to at least try "to gain market

74

share"… by lowering prices when selling "wholesale" crude oil. Or described more crudely (no pun intended), crude oil producers are not trying "to steal" customers from other large oil producers by lowering the price of their own high profit crude oil.

AN OIL COMPANY "PRICE WAR": A (TRULY) HYPOTHETICAL EXAMPLE

To further explain this lack of competition, consider this hypothetical, perhaps oversimplified, but still very relevant example. Sometime, during the last 5 to 10 years, company executives of one of the large international oil companies, Exxon for example, decide to steal customers from other large international oil companies. They intend to do this by at least temporarily lowering gas prices. As described earlier, to lower retail gas prices, oil producers will have to first cut the price that they are charging refineries and brokers, etc. for the crude oil they have produced. As a result of Exxon Corporation charging less for its crude oil, Exxon gas stations in most areas of the country could then, in short order, reduce the price of a gallon of Exxon gas by say 30 cents to $1.00 per gallon. Before other major international gas retailers begin to lower their gas prices in order to compete with Exxon, Exxon gas sales would have surged.

In the end, Exxon, by accepting "less profit per sale", might actually increase total gas sales for the quarter, enough to actually increase total quarterly profits, compared with the previous quarter. Beyond that, Exxon would create an incredible amount of "good will" for their company as citizens throughout America clearly understand (and remember) which oil company broke ranks with the other large oil companies and dramatically lowered retail prices for their gasoline.

"BUT WAIT…I DON'T LIKE COMPETITION"

Large oil company shareholders, oil company executives and other actual wealthy owners of numerous oil wells may prefer the status quo of the past twelve years. They might prefer that virtually all major producers of crude oil continue to charge (and receive) roughly the same high prices for their product (produced crude oil). I understand completely, but unfortunately such cozy pricing policies may border on collusion or price fixing and are possibly illegal. For over 32 years, many times I wanted to charge higher prices for various "high profit products", but always, as noted earlier, there seemed to be another store in the mall or across the street willing to sell the same product for a lower price. (I think it's called "free market capitalism".)

THEIR SILENCE…SPEAKS VOLUMES

It is my sincere opinion that large oil producers have gotten away with a blatant lack of competition between themselves, first and foremost because of the Presidents in charge during the past 12 years. President Bush, of course, was from oil rich Texas. He had many friends and "donors" in the oil business. (Ditto VP Dick Cheney.) During their eight years in office, winks, nods and big smiles were likely the rule among big oil company executives.

President Obama and his Energy Secretary during the previous four years made no serious attempts to substantially bring down gas prices. President Obama is a longtime supporter of so called "alternative energy sources", which of course become more popular when the price of gasoline and other fuel is high. Before being appointed Energy Secretary, Steven Cho reportedly said that he was actually in favor of higher fuel prices. The new, recently appointed Energy Secretary also shows little appetite for confronting potentially "non-competing" oil companies

In addition, during the past 12 years, Congressional majorities, have shown little interest in confronting large oil producers regarding the possible lack of competition. Not since the late seventies has a President and Congress effectively challenged the lack of competition between oil producing companies.

To be sure, there are a few Congressional members, typically Democrats and more liberal Congressional members, who are more than willing to confront oil company executives (as well as crude oil speculators). The arguments of such Congressional members are worthy of in depth media coverage (remember high gas and diesel fuel prices are making life miserable for millions of Americans). However, in the absence of such media coverage, Congressional majorities rule the day.

THE TWO STEP PLAN: A QUICK REVIEW

So again, to quickly review, ten years of artificially high gas prices are largely the result of two factors. The first factor involves big time speculators "betting" and eventually overwhelming the crude oil futures market. The second factor (causing high fuel prices) is a general lack of vigorous competition between crude oil producers within the oil industry during the last eight to ten years. (A third, less important factor, will be discussed in later chapters.)

My solution for dealing with speculators is promoting the notion of a "complete ban" of speculation in the crude oil futures market. My solution for the lack of serious competition in the oil industry is once again to encourage millions of likeminded Americans to demand that Congress take action, by forcing oil company executives (and their accountants) to prove that they have been adequately competing. So, in effect, I am proposing a solution that will potentially bring down gasoline prices that involves two steps to deal with two different problems.

FORCING COMPETITION: WHEN CRUDE OIL PRICES ARE HIGH

To be sure, I am not suggesting the typical "photo opt session" of recent years where executives from a few of the very large oil companies appear before Congressional committees for a day or two and answer questions from Congressional committee members. These executives then board their planes back to Texas, Oklahoma or wherever and nothing of significance really happens. These "question and answer sessions" before Congressional committee members are about as meaningful as the various study groups and panels established by the Commodity Futures Trading Commission in attempts to "better regulate" the financial services sector and its crude oil speculators.

THE KEYS: A CONFRONTATIONAL APPROACH AND PUBLICITY

What we should demand is that Congress and/or the Energy Department Secretary, assemble a group of widely acknowledged experts regarding oil company operations. Large multi-national oil companies, as well as other large oil producing companies in America, would then be required to send similar experts, as well as executives, and spend a week, 10 days, two weeks or whatever it takes to decide whether sufficient competition has been occurring within the oil industry currently and during the last ten years.

The venue for such a gathering of experts could be the traditional Congressional committee hearing rooms. A better choice might be a "Competition Conference" to take place at a larger facility with ample room for interested spectators, reporters, camera men, and of course the participants at the conference. Presumably, the Conference would receive a large degree of publicity and media coverage.

Again, the expanded committee hearings or the so called "Competitive Conference" would be unique because the proceedings would, no doubt, be very confrontational and provide in depth, ongoing debates on key issues regarding competition between crude oil producers. Both defenders and detractors would have ample time to make their case and answer tough questions. At the end of the day, at the end of the week, or by the end of the month, it should be abundantly clear whether or not crude oil producers are adequately competing with one another.

Also, large multi-national oil corporations should be immediately prohibited from paying dividends or buying back company stock, until their respective executives and accountants have convinced the government (and its citizenry) that adequate competition is indeed taking place within the industry. Large oil company producers may need a considerable amount of cash, if they are not able to prove that they have been legitimately competing with one another during the past ten or twelve years.

I am, for sure, not an expert in oil company operations. I simply recognize competition or the potential lack thereof. Perhaps in the weeks ahead, oil company accountants and executives can prove that oil company competition is sufficient. For example, maybe oil company executives can prove that they are not virtually all relying (very conveniently) on the crude oil futures market, to price their crude oil, while virtually ignoring the actual cost of bringing a barrel of crude oil to the surface. This cost is sometimes estimated to be on average maybe $20 per barrel. Given the circumstances, the burden of proof should rest with oil company executives and their accountants.

In July of 2008, the price of crude oil rose to $147 per barrel on the crude oil futures market. Still, gas prices at various large retailers like Exxon and BP, as well as smaller gas retailers in the Atlanta area all remained roughly the same, which was somewhere between $4.10 to $4.25 per gallon of regular gas.

A very relevant question then, to be asked of the above-mentioned oil company accountants and executives is this. How high would crude oil futures prices have to go before Atlanta area commuters could logically expect to see some sign of true competition; that is, for example, gas prices at the gas stations of one of the large international oil companies, being at least occasionally, dramatically lower, perhaps overnight, than those prices charged by gas stations of other large oil companies? Will it in effect never happen, even if crude oil futures prices eventually rise to $300 per barrel?

So for me, it's not just that crude oil prices are almost certainly artificially high and as a result oil producers are making excess profits per barrel. The equally distressing fact is that there is no apparent attempt by the various oil companies to use this excess profit margin to dramatically lower gas prices (at least temporarily) in an attempt "to steal" customers from other gas retailers (as described above).

FORCING COMPETION...WHEN CRUDE OIL PRICES ARE FALLING

It is interesting that in the days ahead, if our two step plan is successful and crude oil futures prices began to fall dramatically, then eventually oil producers will have less opportunity to generate excess or so called "windfall" profits that have been occurring in recent years. In other words, as the (ever changing) world wide price of crude oil continues to decline, the price for a barrel of crude oil could eventually approach the actual cost of bringing a barrel of crude oil to the surface. As noted earlier, this was the situation during most of the 1980's and l990's, when a barrel of crude oil sometimes sold for as little as $8.00 per barrel.

Thus, in the days ahead, instead of focusing on potential "excess" profits within the oil industry, our focus might be on the "crude oil/gasoline price ratio". For example, if crude oil prices eventually fall to $30 per barrel, then we and Federal regulators would have to watch closely to see if indeed gas prices "come down" to levels that would be associated with $30 per barrel crude oil.

As the price of crude oil futures are bid up, oil companies, as described, are all too willing to then raise the price of their gasoline. When the price of such crude oil futures go down, then (with very few exceptions) historically gas prices eventually go down. (This phenom might be crudely described as "the rules of the game" in establishing "gasoline prices").

In the future, if "banning speculators" results in $30 per barrel crude oil, it is "these exceptions" we will be looking for. Simply put, if large oil producers are going to force gas prices up when crude oil futures prices are increasing, then they <u>must</u> force gas prices down when crude oil futures prices are falling.

FORCING COMPETITION...WHEN "THE RULES OF THE GAME ARE CHANGED"

As noted earlier, for many years I drove to Central or South Florida to hand pick and purchase indoor tropical plants for resale. I would (completely) fill a 318 Dodge Van and a 24 foot long trailer with indoor tropical plants. On the 450 to 700 mile trip back to Atlanta, the Dodge Van would average around 5 miles per gallon (if not driving against northwesterly winds).

These trips were quite profitable as long as gas prices were low. Fortunately, as mentioned earlier, gas prices during the 80's and 90's averaged around 80 cents per gallon.

Eventually, I began ordering plants "over the phone" from a plant broker who lived in Orlando, Florida. Still, over the years, if the price of gas began to rise, then my broker had no choice but to add a "gas surcharge" onto his invoice, to help offset his increased fuel prices.

Beginning around 2006, while writing various articles, and more recently a book complaining about high gasoline prices, I have continued to keep almost daily tabs on the going price of crude oil versus the going price of gasoline. Possibly, during the past 35 years, relatively few individuals in the world have kept up with the daily or weekly trends of the ever-changing prices of crude oil and gasoline, more than I have. Thus, perhaps I am qualified to make the following observation.

AN OBSERVATION...FROM A (OBVIOUSLY BORED) SENIOR CITIZEN

Something of historic proportions occurred during, roughly speaking, the first two months of 2013. During a 40 day period, approximately January 20 to March 1st of 2013, the price of gasoline rose dramatically, while the price of a barrel of crude oil remained relatively stable. On or around January 20, 2013, the price of a gallon of regular gas in the suburbs of Atlanta was approximately $3.15 per gallon. On March 1st, the price of regular gas at the same pumps was roughly $3.80 per gallon for regular gasoline. I do not ever remember such a dramatic 40-day rise in gas prices in the face of relatively stable crude oil prices.

Over the past 35 years, rises and declines in gas prices do not, of course, perfectly correlate with rises and declines in crude oil prices. Hurricanes in the Gulf of Mexico, refinery explosions, and other brief "quirks" can cause temporary increases in U.S. gas futures prices and retail gas prices that are greater than the increase in crude oil futures prices. In addition, gas prices vary from state to state and even vary sometimes within a state. Also, crude oil prices can vary from one part of the country to another part of the country.

Still, historically speaking, the overall correlation between gas price changes and crude oil price changes is relatively high. What is almost unprecedented (if my memory serves me well) about the gas price increases in question, is the percent of increase in gas prices over a 40-day period without a significant rise in crude oil prices. The per cent increase approached 20% in less than two months.

RULES OF THE GAME:
AN EXPLANATION

During the past ten years, it has been personally very frustrating as I have watched crude oil (and gas) prices typically rise to unrealistically high levels, because of the "betting" of crude oil speculators and a general lack of competition between oil producers. The only small consolation for me, over the years, was that when crude oil prices were steady, then gas prices were relatively steady. If crude oil prices occasionally fell by 20%, then large oil producers would (probably reluctantly) eventually lower their gas prices by roughly 20%...I refer to such correlating price swings as the "rules of the game" for determining gas prices, in effect for many, many years. (There was a brief period in 2008 as crude oil prices were collapsing from $147 to $32 per barrel, that gas prices "quit dropping" even though crude oil prices continued to fall. This was one of the exceptions I mentioned earlier.)

In previous sections of this chapter, I have discussed the need to force oil producers to compete in two distinct situations. First, they must adequately compete when crude oil prices are rising or are otherwise artificially high. Secondly, oil producers must be forced to compete when crude oil prices are falling or otherwise low.

OIL COMPANIES (IN TANDEM OF COURSE)...IGNORING "THE RULES"

Based on the "unexplained" or otherwise "weakly explained" dramatic gas price increases during the first two months of 2013, a third category needs to be added. Oil producers must be forced to compete "when they change the longstanding rules of the game" and simply raise gasoline prices for a couple of months regardless of the price of crude oil. (As I have stated repeatedly, since crude oil costs are the primary cost of making gasoline, then the going price of gasoline should almost always reflect the going price of crude oil).

Regarding the 40 days in question, it is almost as though speculators in the gas futures markets and oil company executives decided, "hey, we are not making enough money, so why don't all of us get together and just raise the price of our gasoline about 20% during the next several months...too heck with what crude oil is selling for. The Federal government is not going to say much of anything. After all, we give out plenty of donations for political campaigns. We spend enough money advertising in newspapers, on TV and on the radio, that complaints from these outlets will probably be minimal. Hey, let's do it."

That such a hypothetical scenario ever occurred is unlikely. Still, at the conference proposed earlier in this chapter (between government officials, crude oil experts and oil company executives), this roughly 40 day period of "unusual gasoline price increases" will surely be fully debated. At such a conference, the defenders of speculators and oil producing executives will likely claim that the rapid gas price increases of the 40 day period in question were caused by various factors, including temporary refinery shutdowns, the " January changeover" to a new formula for the "summer blend" of gasoline, gasoline futures speculation, etc.

Perhaps, these "high gas price defenders" can successfully make their case. At this point, however, I am skeptical. A 40 day long, small increase in such gas prices... maybe. A "weakly explained" 40 day long, 20% increase in gas prices...sorry I am not buying it."

Maybe the 40 day period of sharply higher gas prices (while crude oil prices were relatively stable) is "a fluke", potentially a one-time occurrence. Nevertheless, it shows a new level of arrogance on the part of oil company executives.

WHAT ABOUT... GASOLINE SPECULATORS?

In addition, "betters" in the U.S. gas futures market have displayed the same degree of arrogance as they helped to drive up gasoline prices for two months,,,without similar price increases in crude oil. In this book, as noted earlier, any time I talk of banning crude oil speculation, my intent is to also "ban" all speculation (that is "betting") in the "gasoline futures market".

These gas price increases of January and February in 2013, are also significant because they illustrate the general ambivalence of most federal politicians and also the Energy Department Secretary with regard to nation-wide sharp rises in the price of gasoline. These "weakly" explained price increases produced, it seems to me, very little response from the Federal government.

Many Americans are frustrated and angered by years of high and unstable gas/fuel prices. However, they feel helpless to do anything about it. The previous pages have outlined a specific plan that Americans can unite behind and thus potentially bring down the price of gasoline. Central to that plan is a Federal government that is more confrontational and more demanding in its dealings with oil company executives (and speculators in the crude oil and gasoline markets). As best I can re-member, the past five U.S. Presidents, the past five (plus) Energy Secretaries and the past 30 years of Con-gressional majorities, have had absolutely no desire to actively confront crude oil producers (or crude oil spec-ulators). That has to change. Adequate competition be-tween oil producers is a must.

ONCE AGAIN...GOVERNMENT INTERFERENCE IN THE AFFAIRS OF PRIVATE BUSINESS

For many years, my wife and I owned and operated retail stores. Thus, as noted earlier I am not generally a fan of the Federal government interfering in the opera-tion of private businesses. For sure, in the case of most industries throughout America, very little reason exists for the Federal government to spend money and time watching for "non-competing businesses". The beautiful thing about <u>true</u> free market capitalism is that "price point competition" virtually always occurs naturally. In fact, the phrase "free market capitalism" is just an empty idiom without the presence of true competition.

However, the situation in the oil industry is very complicated. Large oil companies frequently sell and buy crude oil simultaneously. In addition, large oil companies sell a product that is used to produce fuel and in turn is an absolute necessity for maybe 80 to 90% of Americans. Thus, when the price of gasoline rises and remains historically high for years, then common sense dictates that the Federal government should indeed spend a little extra time and money to guarantee that oil producers are not colluding with one another to, in effect, keep fuel prices unrealistically high.

LEFT WING…"OIL COMPANY HATERS"

Despite my criticism, I am not a "left wing hater" of "Big Oil". As a former business owner, it is easy to imagine the logistic difficulties and various headaches involved in simultaneously buying, selling, exploring for and producing crude oil in various locations throughout the world.

I am impressed by the efficiency with which the oil companies keep all the various gas retailers supplied with gas. I typically buy gas from a nearby gas station that has over 20 gas pumps. It is not unusual to find 80% of those pumps being used at any given time. It is easy to imagine the chaos that would ensue if a disruption to the flow of gasoline should occur, be it the result of a refinery explosion, labor union strikes, hurricanes, etc. Cars would be backed up for miles simply trying to buy a few gallons of gas. Oil company executives have to be always prepared for such potential emergencies.

Also, I have no problem in general with oil producers receiving federal tax breaks and credits on the various costs of exploring for and producing crude oil. (These tax breaks should be reviewed yearly to ensure that they are reasonably effective.) When oil is discovered and brought to the surface by an American company, we as Americans all stand to eventually benefit (provided, of course, oil companies are competing with each other).

In addition, if our "two- step plan" to reduce gas prices in America succeeds, then oil producers will make less profit and may well need some extra incentive to drill for oil. (Most Americans do not remember that all profitable businesses, large and small, were eligible for a 10% investment tax credit until the year 1986. From 1977 until 1986 the investment tax credit saved the middle class type business, that my wife and I owned and operated, thousands of dollars, and for sure, was a positive factor when deciding to expand our single retail location eventually to multiple locations. However, in October of 1986, Congress passed the infamous 1986 Tax Reform Bill which eliminated the investment tax credit, retroactively back to January 1, 1986. On September 8th, 1986, The Atlanta Journal published an article I wrote regarding the tax reform legislation and its negative impact on middle class business owners and middle class farmers.)

Finally, as noted earlier, the examples used in this chapter to illustrate the lack of competition in the oil industry are oversimplified. For example, even during the good economic times of the last ten years, Exxon, for example, would have a more difficult (but not impossible) job of temporarily lowering the price of Exxon gas across much of America, than would, for example, Delta have in lowering its non-stop fares by 30% on all flights from Atlanta to 12 different American cities, at various times during the 1990's when jet fuel was cheap. Nevertheless, the simplified examples I have used are relevant and make the necessary points.

CHAPTER SIX

OIL COMPANY DEFENDERS: SOME STANDARD ARGUMENTS

Just as investment bankers and brokers have many defenders regarding their "speculation" in the crude oil commodities market, so too do oil company executives and oil well owners have many defenders, using a standard set of arguments, against accusations that oil companies are not sufficiently competing. I will quickly discuss several of these arguments.

ARGUMENT NO 1: LOW "NET PROFIT PERCENTAGE"

One widely used argument by pro oil company defenders goes like this, "Bob, you don't understand. Large oil companies have made a lot of money during the last ten years but if you consider their typical net profit percentages each year, then you will see these percentages are quite low."

SPECIAL NOTE: So, what is the "net profit percentage"? The net profit percentage of a company is the total yearly net profit (in dollars) divided by the total yearly sales (in dollars). Described differently, the "net profit percentage" for a given company is the portion of each sales dollar that ends up as "bottom line net profit". "For example, a ten percent net profit percentage (for a company) during the year would mean that ten cents out of every sales dollar is actual net profit. Higher net profit percentages reflect more "bottom-line" profit being generated from each dollar of sales.

The oil company defenders mentioned above might continue by arguing that a particular large international oil company made only ten cents of net profit on each dollar of sales during 2012. The fact that the company made 50 billion dollars in profit last year would be a reflection of its size, not its propensity "to gouge". (By the way, 50 billion dollars is a million dollars in bottom line profit made 50,000 times in one year).

This ten cents figure is lower than "the net profit on each dollar of sales," for various other companies and industries. For example, the average "bottom line" net profit percentage for another industry might be 14%. The defenders of big oil companies argue that oil company executives and, of course, investors (hedge funds, equity funds, and millions of other stock holders) have "a right" to expect a fair return on their investment. Thus, ten cents of profit per dollar of sales is a fair return.

MY RESPONSE: This argument may seem logical at first. However, here are at least four inconsistencies in the argument.

1. No oil company executive or stock holder has "a right" to receive a fair return on their investment (higher dividend rates, etc.). Rather private equity funds and

other investors purchase stocks or the bonds of companies that they "expect" will produce good returns and high dividends. There are no guarantees. Competition driven free market forces should ultimately play a large role in determining returns on investments.

2. Examining the "net profit per dollar of sales figure" is very useful in evaluating the operation of any business. However, this figure alone, if it is relatively low, does not prove that a given company is adequately competing with regard to its pricing policies. Various other factors influence this percentage. For example, failure to control business expenses or failure to maximize (profit producing) company sales, can produce a low "net profit percentage" at the end of the year.

During the many years that my wife and I owned retail stores we always had a high (typically over 40%) yearly gross profit percentage (the percentage calculated by considering only the delivered cost of goods sold). However, our yearly net profit percentage (which considers all business expenses) was virtually always much lower than the 10% figure mentioned above for some of the large international oil companies.

Our company's yearly "net profit percentages" were (unfortunately) always low, because we simply could not generate enough extra sales volume (which as noted, typically produced 40 cents of gross profit per dollar of sales) to adequately cover the hundreds of thousands of dollars of yearly business expenses (rent, wages, utilities, etc.). This lack of yearly sales volume dramatically lowered our yearly "net profit" percentage.

As it turns out, the pricing policies of our retail stores were very competitive. However, the fact that at the end of the year we were only making perhaps "4 cents of bottom line net profit for every dollar of sales", considered by itself, as explained, is not proof of our competitiveness. Neither is an oil company's "ten per cent figure" for their yearly "net profit percentage", necessarily proof of the company's competitiveness.

3. My concern is not simply with the degree of competition between the six or eight largest multinational oil companies. Thousands of medium size oil well owners and producers (sometimes with multi-millionaire owners) should also have to prove that they have, in recent years, adequately competed. My guess is that the so called yearly "net profit percentages" of these companies might be considerably higher than the "net profit percentages" of the large international oil companies. After all, in some cases, these oil well companies are receiving $90 for a barrel of crude oil, obtained from the exact same wells that, during the 1980's and 1990's, they may have been receiving only $20 (or less) per barrel.

4. Finally, defenders of big oil companies should temporarily put aside their stat sheets, net profit percentage figures, etc. and instead answer in straightforward, common sense language a simple question: How do the pricing policies of oil producers from 1982 to 1999 compare with their pricing policies during the last 10 years?

As discussed, during this earlier time period, crude oil prices on the crude oil futures market were quite low (as were gas prices), yet no large multi-national oil companies went bankrupt. In fact, they typically managed to make millions of dollars each year. During this time frame, no one else would expect "slashing" of gasoline prices to occur. Profit margins during the 1980's and 1990's were indeed too small for an oil company to try and increase market share by lowering prices.

During recent years however, the situation is drastically different. Again, this crude oil, sometimes coming from the same oil wells used in the 1980's and 90's, is now during the past ten years, selling for 4, 6, maybe 8 times more than what it sold for during the 1980's and 1990's. Now (and during the previous ten years), with extra gross profit available, is a time we need a few oil company executives with a "Southwest Airlines" or "Walmart" type mindset.

ARGUMENT NO 2:   MIDDLE CLASS OIL INDUSTRY JOBS

A second relative argument used by the defenders of crude oil producers (and speculators) goes like this: Substantially lower crude oil and gas prices will result in less oil company profits, which will in turn result in a large number of jobs being lost in the oil industry.

MY RESPONSE: This assertion is partially true. Some good paying, middle class jobs will, at least temporarily, likely be lost if fuel prices fall dramatically, particularly in the oil exploration and drilling sectors of the industry.

In addition, smaller companies catering to the oil industry will suffer a decline in business. For example, restaurants, companies making temporary housing for oil field exploration workers, and other such small and medium size businesses may be negatively impacted. They may even have to lay off some employees.

The potential loss of such jobs is saddening. However, the alternative, continuing high and unstable gas prices, is distressing as well. Years of high and unstable gas prices have been disastrous to millions of business owners, as well as depleting tens of millions of dollars of disposable income from less prosperous and middle class families. Many, many jobs have been lost because of high fuel prices (as explained in Chapter 7 and elsewhere). On the other hand, low and stable fuel prices will act as an economic stimulant and eventually a job creator for most sectors of the economy.

If gas prices fall dramatically, no large international oil company is going out of business anytime soon. As mentioned repeatedly, crude oil and gasoline prices were relatively low during most of the 1980's and virtually all of the 1990's. Oil companies survived, and in fact, many of them, year after year still made millions of dollars. Also, it should be noted that low gas prices typically result in an overall increase of gas consumption. This increase may induce some sectors of the oil industry to add employees, which will help offset a potential decline in the number of oil workers exploring for oil and building new oil wells.

Finally, even if our two-step plan is completely successful, and gas prices drop dramatically, no guarantee exists that gas prices will remain permanently at low levels. My hope is that dramatically lower and stable fuel prices will be around for an extended period of time, at least five or ten years. This would allow many small and medium size businesses to become economically more viable, and it would of course, help middle class Americans to replenish their stores of disposable income. Still in the months ahead, oil prices could once again rise dramatically, if in fact a true shortage of crude oil occurs.

ARGUMENT NO 3:   HIGH GAS PRICES
HELP PROTECT ENVIROMENT

Many well-intentioned constituents and some Democratic Congressional members "support high gas prices" as a way of cutting gas consumption and in particular, as a way of getting "gas guzzling" vehicles off of the highway. This in turn would cut down on carbon emissions and promote a healthier environment. My daughter and some of her friends share this sentiment. For example, after reading the book, she noted that she was more concerned over the possibility that speculators were driving up the price of food staples, than she was over the possibility that speculators were forcing up gas and diesel fuel prices.

MY RESPONSE: Millions of working Americans, sometimes with families, simply cannot currently afford to buy a more fuel efficient car. In addition, high gasoline prices are economically hammering millions of small business owners. Rather than supporting high gas prices while so many Americans are unemployed or under-employed, why not instead support federal legislation that imposes a significantly high federal tax on the sticker price of a wide range of newly purchased "gas guzzler" type vehicles. This tax could be made high enough to dramatically slow down the sale of such vehicles and perhaps eventually end the production of some vehicles. The revenue from such a tax could be used to promote environmental initiatives.

ARGUMENT NO 4:
ENERGY INDEPENDENCE

A final argument (to be discussed) that is used against those of us who promote lower crude oil and gas prices, focuses on "energy independence". Oil company producers and their defenders will argue that $30 per barrel crude oil and $1.25 per gallon gasoline will make America <u>less</u> energy independent in the days ahead. Their argument essentially is that, as crude oil prices fall dramatically, we will import more crude oil from other countries, and thus become less "energy independent".

MY RESPONSE: I, like virtually all citizens, agree that America needs to become energy independent (or close to it). However, my position is that the amount of crude oil that America imports in a given month, taken by itself, is a simplistic and inappropriate way to gauge whether America is becoming energy independent. In the paragraphs that follow, I will show that such increased crude oil imports do <u>not</u> necessarily make our country less energy independent. Rather, these increased oil imports could make America potentially more energy independent…when it really matters.

CAPPED OIL WELLS: AMERICA'S LOW COST STRATEGIC RESERVES

If the price of crude oil in Canada, Saudi Arabia and other countries falls below the cost of bringing crude oil to the surface at various oil wells (for example in West Texas), then of course, based on the profit driven laws of supply and demand, oil companies will frequently import the cheaper oil (that will eventually be refined into fuel).

During the 1980's and 1990's, many American oil wells were <u>temporarily</u> capped for this very reason, as $10 to $15 crude oil frequently became available. So the question is this. In the long run, does the fact that America saves some of its own crude oil, when thousands of American oil wells are "<u>temporarily</u>" capped, increase or decrease the ability of America to be energy independent during a period when a true energy crisis or a Mideast War causes oil prices to skyrocket?

Or alternatively, assume that during the next 50 years, that there are no such wars or otherwise "truly dramatic" oil shortages. Further assume, that after 50 years or so, the price of crude oil begins to rise dramatically, because the worldwide supply of crude oil really, really is beginning to "run out". Under such a scenario, would capped oil wells (from time to time) during the 50-year period, make America more or less energy independent in 2063?

In both situations, the answer is that (temporarily) capped oil wells <u>increase</u> America's "energy independence" during times when such independence is most important. Such "capping" allows America to conserve a commodity that is an absolute necessity, until economic conditions warrant widespread "uncapping" of America's capped oil wells.

Currently, America maintains four "manmade" Strategic Petroleum Reserves (SPR) located in four sites on the Gulf of Mexico, which Presidents from time to time, "dip into" in order to temporarily hold down rising crude oil prices. In reality, "capped" oil wells are a "naturally stored reserve" of crude oil to be used when prices rise due to a variety of reasons. If crude oil futures prices fall dramatically in the days ahead, and consequently many other countries are willing to sell their crude oil at cheap prices, then (in my view) by all means, buy and use their crude oil to make our gasoline, diesel and jet fuels. Save America's crude oil for use in times of emergencies or dramatically rising oil prices.

GUAGING ENERGY
INDEPENDENCE: AN ALTERNATIVE
METHOD

When it comes to gauging America's level of "energy independence", particularly as it relates to crude oil then, it seems to me, this level could be most accurately measured in this manner. First, regarding <u>consumption</u>, assume that a true energy crisis exists, (perhaps prompted by an all-out war in the Middle East). Further assume that as a result of such a situation, crude oil prices reach unprecedented levels. With these assumptions as a given, then government officials could calculate how much crude oil America currently uses each day and also carefully calculate how much less daily crude oil this country "could get by with" temporarily if a true state of emergency existed.

Then regarding production, government policy makers could calculate the total amount of crude oil that America is capable of producing each day. This production figure would include the amount of crude oil currently being produced from "active" oil wells, as well as the amount of oil that could be produced in the near term from wells that have been capped or otherwise, temporarily, are not producing crude oil. To this figure, government officials could add crude oil production expected to come "online" in the near future as "deep water" wells, various oil pipelines, etc. are completed.

Once this potential crude oil production figure is calculated, then policy makers could subtract the figure from the total number of barrels of crude oil that America must have each day in a crisis situation. Any short fall of daily crude oil consumption needs, could then be analyzed by Federal government decision makers. Factors like the amount of crude oil that America could import daily from "friendly" nearby countries like Canada and Mexico, would be considered, etc.

ARTIFICALLY HIGH FUEL PRICES: ONE "LONELY" WIDESPREAD BENEFIT

Ten years of <u>artificially</u> high crude oil prices have produced at least one positive that will eventually prove beneficial to most Americans. The "artificially" increased prices of crude oil have motivated oil producers to invest extra money into exploring for and actually building oil wells capable of producing more crude oil. The ensuing substantially increased production of crude oil in America and off the coast of America, has unfortunately not translated into noticeably significant declines in current fuel prices in America. However, in the days ahead, such exploration for and discoveries of crude oil eventually will economically benefit most Americans.

If our "two-step plan" is successful and crude oil prices fall back to the $25 to $40 dollar per barrel range, then, for sure, all oil company exploration and oil well building, is not simply going to suddenly end. Oil companies, with millions of dollars already invested in various projects, will likely complete most of such projects, even if they temporarily have "to cap" production at such facilities. Oil company executives and oil well owners know that crude oil prices can rise as quickly as they fall. A drop in crude oil prices to $30 per barrel may temporarily slow down exploration and production of crude oil in America, but it will not end it.

CRUDE OIL EXPLORATION
AND PRICES...DOWN THE ROAD

Oil well owners, oil company executives, and oil company investors, economically speaking, have had a very, very "nice run" during the last ten years. My hope is that our plan to end crude oil speculation and to also return competition driven, free market capitalism into the production, pricing and selling of crude oil, will in effect keep crude oil prices, and thus fuel prices relatively low for many years. However, only time will tell.

Very soon after "speculation" is banned, true crude oil competition returns, and crude oil prices fall, various oil producing cartels, particularly OPEC, will try to implement other "anti-capitalistic" measures to once again force up crude oil prices. These cartels will try to force member countries to limit the production of crude oil and thus potentially produce "artificial" shortages of crude oil. Such efforts to limit production occurred during much of the 1980's and 1990's. These efforts had only limited success. As noted often, crude oil prices remained cheap during most of the 1980's and virtually all of the 1990's.

Crude oil production and consumption is a huge business. Potential daily profits are enormous. Oil company executives and oil well owners, large and small, understand that even in the absence of "speculation", crude oil prices, as noted earlier, could again rise significantly. The exploration for and the production of this so-called "black gold" will always be around as long as undiscovered or undeveloped crude oil exists.

So federal policy makers and/or oil producers cannot rightly argue that crude oil prices (and thus gasoline prices) <u>must</u> be kept artificially high (via speculation, lack of oil company competition, etc.) because of the need for "energy independence". Such a federal government policy would, conveniently enough, economically benefit oil producers at the expense of other businesses and middle class families (as I have argued previously). Indeed, such policy makers should allow competition driven, free market capitalism to once again determine crude oil prices. If deemed necessary, these Federal decision makers can propose, debate and vote on additional Federal legislation to encourage use of alternative energy sources or encourage increased oil company exploration, in order to promote "energy independence".

A QUICK REVIEW...AND ALTERNATIVE SOLUTION

Now, before moving on to Part Three of the book (beginning with Chapter 7), I would like to quickly summarize the past six chapters. The situation is as follows. You, I and thousands of millions of individuals around the world are negatively impacted by high and unstable fuel prices. Gas prices are hugely influenced by the ever changing daily price of crude oil sold in the crude oil futures and swaps market.

So we are all counting on this market to accurately establish a <u>realistic</u> and <u>true</u> price for a barrel of crude oil; that is, the crude oil price should be a response to the supply and demand dynamics that create prices for millions of other items for sale worldwide. That is pretty much what the crude oil futures market did….until the last ten years or so.

As described, politically connected investment bankers and other wealthy active investors helped convince Congress in December of 2000, to finalize their ongoing efforts to deregulate the oil markets (and other markets as well), in effect "changing the rules" regarding speculation. This, in turn, made it easier and safer for speculators to place huge bets in the crude oil futures market, with frequently only 10% down, simply on whether the price of crude oil would go up or down in the days ahead. It is my opinion that the crude oil futures market has been "screwed up" ever since, and in the process has "screwed up" the lives of millions of small business owners and middle class families throughout America (and the world) during the last 10 years.

Many influential individuals recognize the potential danger of such speculation. Almost always their solution is to "better regulate" this betting. In other words, these multi-millionaires can keep on betting, "just better regulate" their speculation.

However, to me the recently gained right to greater speculate is so absurd, so opposed to the "greater good" and so anti-capitalistic, that the "very right" to place such bets should be legally denied. In other words, crude oil (and gasoline) speculation should be banned completely. Forget all notions of so called "better regulating" speculation.

This complete ban should produce dramatically falling crude oil prices followed by falling fuel prices. All that is left then, in order to maximize the drop in gas and other fuel prices, is an absolute "guarantee" from the federal government that oil companies will be forced to adequately compete with one another.

Most of us live and coexist in a politically correct and civilized world. My proposal of a complete ban on crude oil speculation reflects this fact. However, in a previous era, not too long ago, the citizenry might favor this alternative solution. "Round up" all wealthy speculators betting in the crude oil futures market (with a clear understanding that their bets are forcing fellow Americans to suffer by paying higher prices for gas), tar and feather them, place them sitting backwards atop a donkey, and then run all of their "rear-ends" out of town.

Similarly, round up all Congressional members who voted in December of 2000 in favor of a greater right for speculators to screw up the crude oil markets (and during the past 12 years have not publicly repented of their wayward ways), and repeat the above process. Ditto all non-competing executives of oil producing companies and non-competing oil well owners. (Attention all Wall Street speculators: Place bets now on the rising price of "donkey futures".)

PART THREE

TOWARD A <u>REAL</u>

ECONOMIC RECOVERY

CHAPTER SEVEN

AN AMERICAN ECONOMIC RECOVERY: A NEW APPROACH

To this point, I have discussed the problem (high fuel prices), a potential two step solution to the problem, and several basic arguments that will be used against our efforts. Before concluding this book however, I need to briefly describe exactly how the federal government's possible role in this "two-step solution" to lower fuel prices, represents an entirely new, potentially bi-partisan approach that Congress and the President could adopt to quickly begin the long awaited true <u>widespread</u> "American economic recovery"

THE KEY: INCREASING MIDDLE CLASS DISPOSABLE INCOME

This new approach requires that the Federal government focus on initiatives that quickly and for sure increase disposable income of middle class Americans

(roughly speaking, individuals or couples making between 25,000 to 125,000 dollars per year). Using this
approach, the ultimate goal is similar to the "stated
goals" of most federal policy makers, that is, maximize
the number of able bodied Americans actually working,
producing, hiring, generating income, paying taxes,
etc. (Disposable income can be increased in at least three
ways, including decreased monthly expenses, increased
monthly earnings or an increase in the availability of
credit.)

CURRENT FOCUS: INCREASE DISPOSABLE INCOME OF INVESTMENT BANKERS AND "ACTIVE" INVESTORS

Currently and during the past five years, the initiatives proposed by the Federal government to help stimulate the economy typically follow a different
approach. Frequently the approach is to immediately
and definitely provide economic benefits to investment
bankers and active wealthy investors, and then hope that
these economic benefits eventually filter down to middle
class and less prosperous families, as well as to middle
class small business owners.

A good example is the massive economic bailout of
Wall Street in 2007 and 2008. During this bailout two
different Presidents, two different Treasury Secretaries
and two different Congressional majorities, as well as
Federal Reserve members and other powerful individuals helped guarantee immediate economic help (cold
cash and credit) for investment bankers and other active
investors. (Many such recipients had helped create the

109

financial market collapse in 2007 and 2008.) Other Americans, including the middle class, were told in effect to wait, and eventually we would all see that the bailout of the financial services sector did indeed benefit all Americans...most of us are still waiting for "houses to start selling again".

An even better example would be the ongoing Q.E. programs of the Federal Reserve during the past four plus years. The Q.E. programs are currently pumping one million dollars into the financial service sector, 85,000 times each month. Supposedly, these huge and immediate cash benefits to investment bankers and other Wall Street types will eventually trickle down to the masses on main street and beyond, in the form of (even) lower interest rates, better job opportunities, blah , blah, blah.

Finally, as discussed in previous chapters, the Federal government essentially produced and has vigorously protected the right of speculators to bet in crude oil and other commodities markets. This gift from the Federal government has proved very, very profitable to many investment bankers and other wealthy investors, but has produced only headaches for middle class citizens trying to work $70 gas fill ups into their monthly budgets.

In recent months, we hear reports that the economic recovery in America has "turned the corner" or is "picking up steam". The unemployment rate is slowly falling and each quarter America manages to produce (unlike many European countries) a small increase in Gross Domestic Product.

Unfortunately, perhaps the most important barometer of America's general economic health, the so called "median household income figure", is dismal indeed. Current reports, which are produced by the U.S. Census Bureau, indicate that recent "household median incomes" have fallen by roughly 7 to 10%, when compared with the same inflation adjusted figures for 2007 (as the financial collapse began), 2003 (10 years ago), or the year 2000 (the beginning of the century). The implications of these figures are staggering. In one of the world's richest countries, tens of millions of its citizens (over a relatively long period of time) are making less money each year.

At the same time, however, they are having to pay increasing prices for many essential goods and services, including gasoline, some food items, healthcare coverage, home owners insurance, college tuition, etc. In addition, the value of these individual's principal asset, their home, has likely fallen by 30 to 40% during the past six years. If you are a politician (or investment banker), don't be in the same room with these folks when you talk about an American economic recovery in high gear. (Interestingly enough, the Wall Street Journal reported on May 18th, 2013, in an article by Tom Orlik, that private-sector wages in China rose 14% in 2012. The article further reported that such wages rose by 12.3% in 2011, with such figures being reported by China's National Bureau of Statistics.)

CHANGING THE FOCUS:
IT'S THE ONLY WAY

What I will propose in the following pages is this. If Congress, the President and Federal Reserve members think that the U.S. economy needs to be stimulated with Federal government cold cash, then such stimulation should be "more balanced" than is currently the case. For example, if Q.E. programs benefitting prosperous investment bankers and wealthy active investors are deemed to be necessary, then similar Federal initiatives should be specifically designed to definitely (and quickly) benefit middle income citizens.

I can easily think of four such Federal initiatives aimed at increasing middle class disposable income. However, a federal initiative (as outlined in this book) that quickly and dramatically lowers fuel prices throughout American is the least expensive, quickest and most obvious way to begin the process of economically energizing the middle class. In fact, the plan outlined in the previous six chapters to quickly bring down fuel prices would actually stimulate the American economy without requiring any Federal government payouts using taxpayer money or credit.

Currently (and unfortunately), the President and most members of Congress would look you in the eye and tell you "there is no way the Federal government can help to quickly and dramatically bring down fuel prices." I say there is a way. In fact, I have of course written this book to outline just such a way. So let us assume that gas prices drop from the current price of

$3.50 per gallon (for regular gasoline in metro Atlanta) down to $1.25 per gallon during the next several months. Here is what we might expect.

Lower and stable gas prices will benefit the vast majority of Americans. However, wealthy and prosperous Americans almost always have a sufficient amount of disposable income. Even poor Americans sometimes (but not always, of course) have a decent amount of disposable income because their monthly expenses are typically low and they sometimes receive significant help from the Federal and State governments.

It is large sectors of middle income America that have been most economically hammered in recent years. Ten years of historically high gas prices, ever increasing healthcare costs, increasing costs for home owner insurance, ever higher college tuition, and the "credit and equity busting" housing collapse have left millions of middle class citizens with little or no monthly disposable income. It is these individuals and families that low gas prices could most benefit.

OPTING FOR "PLAN B": SHRINKING THE MIDDLE CLASS

Currently, many such middle income families continue to "hang on", pay their bills, and hope for better economic opportunities. However, each day some middle class individuals will, at least temporarily, give up on the so called "American dream". They will instead opt for "Plan B". I myself know of several such individuals.

Many of these individuals (opting for Plan B) worked hard during much of their adult lives. They may have been living "paycheck to paycheck" but they owned a home, maybe raised a family and typically (with the help of charge cards and equity lines of credit) paid their bills. Then something happens. It could be the loss of a job that provided decent health care coverage, reduction of credit lines, maybe the onset of a chronic illness or a middle class small business owner who simply "throws in the towel". Eventually, many of these individuals make a conscious effort to leave the ranks of the middle class and opt for Plan B. Under "Plan B", they will likely qualify for food stamps, government subsidized housing, Medicaid and other state and federal programs.

In short, these individuals sometimes cease to be productive tax-paying citizens. In so doing, they quit making mortgage payments. In some states it takes up to two years or longer to foreclose and evict someone from their home; potential savings: perhaps $1,000 per month. They quit paying their monthly minimum payment on their charge cards; potential saving: perhaps $400 per month. They quit repaying their home owner's equity line of credit; potential savings: perhaps $300 per month. They become eligible for food stamps, subsidized housing and Medicaid; potential savings: perhaps $500 per month. Finally, many such individuals will better qualify for the "Earned Income Tax Credit" each year, which can be paid "in advance". The value of such earned income credits might range from say $200 to $5,000 per year.

REVERSING THE TREND: THE FIRST STEP

So, "$1.25 per gallon gas" sometime next month would quickly have a positive economic impact on America's middle class, and eventually America as a whole, in at least three ways. $1.25 per gallon gas would:

1. Improve economic conditions and job opportunities in the middle class sector (as explained momentarily) which would eventually encourage less prosperous and poor Americans to actively seek out "middle class type jobs"…and "give up" many of the "Plan B" government benefits mentioned above. Also, this increase in job opportunities would slow down the current exodus of potentially productive citizens from the middle class ranks and into the ranks of those qualifying for Medicaid, food stamps, subsidized housing, etc. In other words, those middle class citizens opting for "Plan B" would slow.

2. Allow tens of millions of middle class families to potentially save $100 to $300 each month resulting from less expensive "gas fill ups". In addition, these families would gain increased disposable income as the prices on various necessities like groceries eventually fall as a result of reduced shipping costs to the grocer or other retailers.

3. Economically benefit the vast majority of American businesses, but relatively speaking, would most positively impact middle class business owners catering primarily to middle income and less prosperous customers.

MIDDLE CLASS STIMULANTS... ARE SMALL BUSINESS STIMULANTS

The case for increasing disposable income for middle class American families is clear enough. However, it is possible that some Federal policy makers simply do not fully understand "the small business connection".

Most experts agree that the key to an American economic recovery is increased hiring by businesses, particularly so called small businesses. It is interesting then, that the vast majority of small business owners are also middle class Americans. So Federal or State government initiatives that directly and clearly economically aid middle class families, typically aid middle class business owner's personal finances similarly.

However, what is important to realize, is that increasing disposable income for middle class families has an economic impact on middle class business owners that is possibly three or four times as great. Consider, for example, the impact of a $1.25 gas versus the current metro Atlanta price of $3.50 per gallon for regular gasoline. Millions of middle class families would likely save more than a $150 a month on gas fill-ups and eventually pay less (as noted) for food and other necessities.

Middle class small business owners and their families would similarly save on such personal expenses. However, in addition, the impact of $1.25 per gallon gas on the profitability of small businesses (and large businesses) within the community would often be profound. Frequently, the delivery cost of goods pur-chased for resale, would significantly decline. Retailers would have the option of lowering everyday prices on such merchandise for resale, thus potentially increasing store traffic, sales and profits. Employees of a business owner would pay less in fuel costs to drive back and forth to work, increasing job satisfaction levels. (If you are making $9.00 or $10.00 per hour, it's a big deal!) Long time customers who have moved perhaps 25–30 miles from a business location, may well fulfill their urge to return to their long time "retail shop hangout" to shop and visit with the owners...if gas is $1.25 rather than $3.50 per gallon.

BUSINESSES REALLY, REALLY NEED... CUSTOMERS WITH DISPOSABLE INCOME

However, the biggest economic positive for small business owners (and executives of large businesses) is the impact on weekly business sales that would result di-rectly from the increase in disposable income of poten-tial customers, created by $1.25 gas. If a typical economically hard pressed middle class family acquires an extra $150 to $200 in monthly disposable income be-cause of low fuel prices, then that money will likely be spent at a local business within the community.

As successful small businesses within the commu-nity begin to see significant rises in retail sales and prof-its, then these business owners will likely purchase more products from other commercial vendors. Eventually these small retailers, wholesalers and distributors will begin hiring new employees from within the community to help handle the increases in sales volume. This additional hiring will result in still more purchasing power for individuals within a community, which produces still more increases in sales and profits for business owners, possibly followed by additional hiring. Eventually, business profits might rise to the point where a small business owner actually decides to open a second location, which will, of course, require still more hiring.

"A JOB CREATING MACHINE"...
WITHIN A COMMUNITY

This "circular process" of increased disposable income leading to increased sales and profits for business owners, leading to increased hiring, leading to even larger increases in disposable income can and does occur. The key (or the spark plug) that is required for this circular job creating machine to "kick in" is ample, widely dispersed disposable income amongst the citizenry within a community.

Many economic and political pundits puzzle over the fact that numerous large corporations with hoards of cash are still not hiring. The reason, I believe, for this lack of hiring is that executives of large corporations realize what many middle class business owners clearly understand. A severe shortage (or complete lack) of widespread disposable income is the case among large swaths of middle class families throughout America. So "the spark plug"; that is, widespread middle class disposable income, benefits both large and small companies.

118

Even if a strong "potential" demand exists for a company's "non-essential" goods or services, a widespread shortage of middle class disposable income frequently limits the possibility of increases in sales and profits from such products. Thus, large businesses (and small businesses) have no reason to hire new employees if increases in current or future sales seem unlikely because of, again, a general lack of widespread disposable income amongst the masses within a community.

I am not simply pontificating about possible ways to create new jobs. I know for a fact that the "job creating machine" really works. I have been there. My wife and I were part of the process for over 32 years. Creating new jobs is just as simple as I have described. The key again…and again, is ample widespread disposable income.

WALL STREET: A "JOB CREATING MACHINE" IN HIGH GEAR

It is interesting that this "job creating machine" can be working quite well in some sectors of the economy while virtually shut down in other sectors. Consider the financial services sector; a sector where relatively few middle class individuals or middle class business owners are actively involved (unless, of course, you are Barak Obama and consider those individuals making $200,000 per year to be members of the middle class).

Investment bankers, stock brokers, hedge fund managers, private equity fund managers, etc. as a group are typically more prosperous than are members of most other business sectors. In addition, the customers actively buying and selling stocks, bonds, commodities, etc. within the financial services sector are typically more prosperous or even wealthy. Thus, not surprisingly, there is plenty of disposable income available in and around Wall Street and other financial sectors nationwide.

This disposable income (and wealth) has been vigorously protected and promoted during the past five years through various "federal government initiatives". A few of these initiatives, as noted earlier, include thousands of millions of dollars in the form of massive monetary bailouts during 2007 and 2008 for investment bankers, commercial bankers and active wealthy investors. In addition, stock market stimulants like "the three trillion dollar Q.E. programs" directly and immediately benefit investment bankers, stock brokers and their clients. Federal government policies that have promoted speculation in the crude oil markets has produced ten years of higher priced gasoline. Directly as a result of these artificially high gasoline prices, a huge influx in recent years of petro dollars into the financial markets has greatly benefitted many investment bankers and their clients.

As a result of this ample disposable income, unemployment rates in the financial services sector are relatively low. Earnings for average stock brokers and investment bankers are typically in the six digit range, profits for investment banks and commercial banks are and have been at historically high levels during recent years. Except for the Nasdaq Exchange, the various

American market indexes have recently repeatedly recorded readings that have easily exceeded their highs of 2007 (before the "crash"). The Dow Jones Industrial average establishes new record highs virtually every week. It is pretty amazing, regarding the positive economic impact that a little extra disposable income can have.

If the Federal government during the last four years, had worked even one fourth as hard to promote increased disposable income throughout middle class America, as it has worked to promote (and protect) disposable income in and around Wall Street and the other financial services sectors nationwide; then America, I truly believe, would currently be enjoying a robust, <u>widespread</u> economic recovery.

<u>REDUCING</u> MIDDLE CLASS DISPOSABLE INCOME: THE PRESIDENT AND CONGRESS IN ACTION

Three years ago, in December of 2010, President Obama and House Speaker, John Boehner, held an oval office meeting to avoid a so called "economic crisis". They emerged from the meeting and announced an agreement that would extend the Bush Era Tax cuts for <u>everyone</u> (including, of course, President Obama and a vast majority of Congressional members) for a period of two years.   The deal also contained other provisions. Most interestingly, a Federal government initiative was included that allowed for a 2% reduction in payroll taxes for all Americans with "earned income", rich or poor, for tax year 2011. (The "2% reduction" was eventually extended by Congress to include tax year 2012).

Thus, an individual who had earned income of $50,000 during 2011, would pay $1,000 less during the year in payroll taxes. An individual who made $106,800 of earned income would save $2,136 because of the 2% cut in Social Security taxes.

On the other hand, an individual that made $200,000, $500,000 or five million dollars of earned income would still only get a $2,136 reduction in payroll taxes owed. The reason is this. Social Security taxes were only withheld from the first $106,800 worth of earned income, during tax year 2012. Thus, the maximum amount of tax savings per year for any individual as a result of the 2% Payroll Tax Deduction Plan, is $2.136 ($106,800 x .02). So clearly this 2% tax cut plan, first initiated in December of 2010, was directed toward and relatively speaking, most benefitted middle income families, which in this book includes families with income of say between $25,000 and $125,000 per year.

More recently, (on January 2, 2013) after much angst, wringing of the hands, finger pointing, etc., President Obama and Congressional leaders concluded negotiations that avoided yet another "economic crisis", the much publicized, so called "fiscal cliff". Had a deal not been reached, the Bush Era Tax cuts would have expired at the end of December, 2012 and many Americans, especially more prosperous Americans, would have received almost a 5% Federal income tax increase beginning in January of 2013.

The final version of the deal established permanent (rather than temporary) tax rates for various groups of citizens. "Left out" in the final version of the deal was the Federal initiative that provided for the 2% cut in payroll taxes discussed above.

The loss of this 2% payroll tax deduction for wage earners, means that in 2013, perhaps over 100 million middle class Americans could potentially bring home a smaller monthly paycheck than they did during the previous two years. Thus, monthly disposable income for such families could potentially decline each month during 2013.

THE PAMPERED SECTOR: FINANCIAL SERVICES AND THEIR CLIENTS

In this Chapter (and throughout the book), I complain that the Federal government, during the past 12 years and especially the last five years, has pampered and protected the economic interests of investment bankers, brokers and active investors, while substantially ignoring the economic plight of most middle class Americans. The "2% reduction in payroll tax initiative" (in effect for tax years 2011 and 2012) was a shining and "lonely" example of a Federal initiative that actually did immediately and for sure benefit virtually all members of the middle class.

The "2% initiative" also benefitted most investment bankers and investors, but relatively speaking not as much as it benefitted middle income Americans. An investment banker making $300,000, $500,000 or 5 million dollars per year may not be impressed that he is going to save $2,136 on payroll taxes. After all, his business sector is receiving the equivalent of one million dollars, 85,000 times each month, from the Federal Reserve via the most recent Q.E. program. Conversely, a middle class couple making $50,000 of earned income with three children may be very grateful for the $1,000 they saved last year on payroll taxes owed.

Investment bankers and wealthier type investors were also likely "displeased" that the 2% payroll tax deduction offered no tax benefit to several classifications of income that frequently accrue to such individuals. Examples of such income would be interest income, dividend income and capital gains income.

PAMPERED INCOMES: DIVIDEND, INTEREST AND CAPITAL GAINS INCOME

The Federal government/IRS classifies income that individuals and "private businesses" generate each year in a variety of ways. Some examples are earned income, capital gains income, interest income, dividend income, Social Security income, etc. These types of income are frequently taxed (or exempted) by the IRS in different ways.

Significantly, only one class of personal income or private business income is required to pay Social Security taxes. That would be so called "earned income". Simply put, if you work for someone and for example receive a paycheck every two weeks, then your earnings are almost always "earned income". If you own a business (as a sole proprietorship) then the Schedule C net income that must be calculated each year is considered to be earned income. Social Security taxes on such earned income are typically deducted from each employee's paycheck. Private employers are expected to pay such Social Security taxes via Estimated Quarterly Federal Government tax payments (at twice the "normal rate").

Capital gains, dividend and interest income have Federal tax rates (and exclusions) that vary. These classifications of income are available to all Americans. However, the vast bulk of these types of income is claimed by investment bankers and prosperous active investors. Since interest income, dividend income and capital gains income are not subject to Social Security taxes, these types of income did not benefit from the 2% reduction in payroll taxes during the past two years. Wealthy investors that are active in the financial markets do not take kindly to being ignored when tax breaks are being doled out.

THE TINY, LONELY TWO PER-CENTER: IN SEARCH OF AN ADVOCATE

The truly remarkable aspect of the "fiscal cliff" deal in the waning days of 2012, was not simply that the 2% payroll tax cut was not extended. Rather, it was the lack of serious support for the initiative from either political party (or the President). Early on, in the final days of negotiations, to avoid "the cliff", it became obvious that neither political party was going to push for inclusion of this tiny, lonely 2% tax cut in the "final package". Actually, including our little bitty 2% payroll tax cut in the final package of tax deals was not even close.

The Democratic Party, long, long, long ago was widely recognized to be the Party of the "working man", the Party of the average American, or the Party of the people. Today, Democratic Party politicians would, no doubt, still claim that mantel. Yet, when it comes time to "stimulate the economy" or promote extra spending power (i.e. disposable income) for the citizenry, most members of the Party apparently would prefer to have the Federal Reserve pump 85,000 million dollars <u>each month</u> into the economy using Q.E. programs, rather than push for the extension of the 2% payroll tax cut.

As I have noted elsewhere, the vast bulk of this Q.E. money stays in one already prosperous business sector; that would be the financial services sector. In addition, some of this Q.E. money actually <u>leaves</u> the country and is invested in the financial markets of other countries. On the other hand, for sure, the small 2% monthly savings resulting from the payroll tax cuts typically stayed and has been spent in communities throughout America.

Then, we have the Republican Party, the Party that promotes the welfare of business, (especially big business and active investors); the Party that claims time and again that tax cuts stimulate and "grow" the economy; the Party that claims that "the people" deserve to keep more of their hard earned money, etc. Yet, in late December and very early January 2013, a majority of Republicans showed no real interest in promoting a tax cut that would have benefitted well over a hundred million Americans.

On the other hand, Republican Congressional leaders were willing "to go to the mat" during the negotiations, to insure that a relatively small group of individuals that make upwards of $400,000 per year would get the same marginal tax rate advantages that those making less than $200,000 were entitled to.

In this chapter I have argued that only one path guarantees a true widespread economic recovery. That path passes directly through middle class America. Such an economic recovery requires that the Federal government promote initiatives that quickly increase the monthly disposable income of tens of millions of middle class families (families earning $25,000 to $125,000 per year). The 2% tax reduction initiative did just that.

The fact that neither political party nor the President actively fought to extend the "2 per center" (for at least one more year), pretty much shows that Federal policy makers simply disagree with my notion that a true widespread economic recovery starts when the "economic sparkplug" is fired; that is, when widespread increases of disposable income occur throughout middle class America. Instead, apparently most (but not all of course) Federal politicians of recent years seem to feel that the road to economic recovery must begin and proceed along Wall Street and the "main drags" of other financial districts in larger cities throughout America.

THE JOB CREATING MACHINE...
IN REVERSE

So, one of the goals of this book is to promote "increases" not "decreases" in middle class disposable income. These increases can "fire up" the job creating machine (as described) nationwide. Unfortunately this circular process leading to increased hiring can and has in recent years, worked "in reverse" in middle class communities throughout America. As disposable income has declined across huge sectors of the middle class, "net hiring" frequently has ended within these communities.

As explained earlier, the price of gasoline dramatically impacts "the job creating machine". Substantially lower fuel prices typically help business owners, particularly middle class business owners, even more than such lower gasoline prices help middle class families. Unfortunately, the converse is usually true as well. For example, rapidly rising, unstable or artificially high gas prices, have even more of a negative impact on most middle-class small business owners, than such high prices have on the "personal" finances of middle class individuals.

$3.75 GAS: A "JOBS VAPORIZER"

As noted at the outset of this book, my wife and I closed our last retail store when the lease expired on May 31st of 2009. The primary reason we closed the store, was due to years of historically high and unstable gas prices, with the prospect of higher and even more unstable gas prices during the years ahead.

It was our feeling that during the three or four year period preceding our store closing, that our regular customers all too frequently did not have the money (or credit) with which to purchase our products as they had previously done. In other words, the desire/demand for our various products (all of which were non-essential) seemed to be roughly the same as it had been for years. Unfortunately, potential customers simply did not seem to have enough disposable income to purchase what they wanted.

Many fellow business owners shared our view, and they themselves were dealing with significant declines in sales volumes. In addition, we had long time customers come to our stores and browse, rather than buy. These customers sometimes shared with us the personal negative economic impact of higher gasoline prices (and higher natural gas prices) on their monthly budgets. These customers also complained of the negative impact of the "housing bust", followed by the subsequent sudden reduction of credit limits on charge cards. In addition, many potential customers during this time period likely decided on various occasions, against even a visit to our local mall because of high gasoline prices.

Federal policy makers, many of whom have never owned a typical middle class business, need to better understand the profound negative impact that artificially high gas prices have on middle class small business owners. Consider, for example, the sum total of gas purchases made during any given daylight hour within a 3-mile range of our last retail store. Each hour, tens of millions of dollars left the pockets and bank accounts of potential customers. Much of this cash in the form of $25, $40 or $80 gas purchases left the community never to return.

Retail gas station's profit margins are very small. The profit margins at oil and gas refineries are not particularly high. So the bulk of the cash from these gas purchases ends up in the hands of oil producers. Individuals and companies in West Texas, Louisiana, Mexico, Canada or the Middle East are receiving the lion's share of the sum total of such gas purchases in your community.

AN OIL RICH SHEIK: WHAT IS HE TO DO?

As an example, consider the plight of an oil rich Sheik, somewhere in Saudi Arabia. During most of the 1980's and virtually all of the 1990's, the Sheik was typically receiving only $10 to $20 for a barrel of crude oil that he owned or controlled. After taking care of his and the extended family's personal needs, perhaps not much money was left over.

Now, during the past 10 years this same Sheik is frequently receiving over $90 per barrel for his crude oil (in July 2008 he may have been receiving $140 per barrel). What is this oil rich Sheik to do with all of this extra cold cash he is receiving for his crude oil? Interest rates at commercial banks in America and many other countries are very low. Thus, almost certainly, our oil rich Saudi Arabian Sheik is going to invest a large chunk of his "petro dollars" with a stock broker or investment banker somewhere in the world. The best we can hope for is that it is an American stock broker.

A similar plight presents itself to the multi-millionaire owner of 300 oil wells somewhere in West Texas, Oklahoma or Louisiana. What is he to do with the additional revenue he is now receiving for the crude oil that his oil wells are methodically producing? Again, a good chance exists that a large chunk (not all of course) of these petro dollars will benefit a stock broker or investment banker at an exchange somewhere in the world.

Thus, eventually a goodly portion of the money you spent for gas last week, ends up being invested in the financial markets somewhere in the world. The financial markets, of course include the commodities markets, which include the crude oil markets. So, petro dollars from your gas purchases last week, not only substantially leave the local community, but they may also be used to speculate in the crude oil markets. Such "betting" (as described repeatedly) can potentially force up the worldwide price of crude oil, which then causes further increases in the price of gasoline and other fuel. Pretty neat, huh…if you are speculating in the crude oil markets or you are an oil company executive (or an owner of oil wells).

So, hopefully it is clear that low and stable gas prices, relatively speaking, will for sure dramatically benefit less prosperous and middle class families and small business owners immediately and will eventually (or simultaneously) significantly benefit virtually all Americans. If the Federal government can, for example, help bring about such a decline in gas prices (as outlined earlier in the two step plan), then it is indeed a worthy endeavor. As noted earlier, I could think of at least three other initiatives that the Federal government could undertake that would quickly and <u>for</u> <u>sure</u> increase disposable income for many millions of Americans.

WHAT ABOUT…SO CALLED "ACTIVE" WEALTHY INVESTORS?

The title of the next chapter is The Financial Services Sector: Middle Class Scapegoat? Thus, now is perhaps a good time to try and quickly clarify a phrase, "active" wealthy investors that I have used (and will continue to use in this book). Specifically, who are these so called "active" wealthy investors? How does an "active investor" differ from a "passive investor"? Why is the distinction necessary?

For the purposes of this book, and generally speaking, an investor is "active" if he or she buys and sells stocks, bonds, commodities or other financial instruments on a regular basis, perhaps hourly, daily or weekly. An "active investor" (1) does not work for one of the big investment banks like Goldman Sachs, (2) may or may not be an investment banker, (3) may invest only personal money or may invest the money of other individuals and (4) is usually, but not always, very prosperous or wealthy. Some examples of such "active investors" are hedge fund managers, equity fund managers, sovereign fund managers, pension fund managers, college endowment funds managers, insurance fund managers and wealthy individuals who simply enjoy regularly "playing the stock market" on their own (or with their favorite stockbroker).

Whether wealthy or not, these "active investors" typically control hundreds of millions of dollars from which they can buy and sell financial products. Frequently, the equities markets of the world move "up and down" in unison. It is typically the decisions of the above described "active investors" (as well as traders from large investment banks) which are primarily responsible for such movement in worldwide financial markets.

WELL WHAT ABOUT... NON-ACTIVE (OR PASSIVE) TYPE INVESTORS?

The phrases "passive" or "non-active" investors are not used in this book, except in this section. Nevertheless, it is important to distinguish between so called "active" and "non-active" investors as the phrases relate to this book. Non active/passive investors far outnumber so-called "active investors". You, the reader, if you are invested in "the markets" are most likely a passive, non-active investor.

Non-active (or passive) investors may have small amounts of money invested in "the markets" or they may have very large amounts invested. Non-active investors do not actively try themselves, to generate profits from their financial investments on an hourly, daily or weekly basis. They do not control or invest the money of other individuals. Worldwide, there are hundreds of millions of passive investors. Many passive/non active investors have invested their money "in the stock market" because the other primary investment alternative, "savings type accounts" at commercial banks, have been typically paying very, very low interest rates (sometimes less than one percent per year) during the past five years...yet another "long term gift" to investment banks from the Federal Reserve.

Some examples of passive, non-active investors would be the tens of millions of individuals with money invested in IRA'S or other retirement accounts. Also included would be individuals with money invested in various money market type funds. Other non-active investors are those who have had money invested in the markets for many years, without ever seriously considering selling such investments in the near term. Many passive investors have very little interest in the daily "ups and downs" of the financial markets.

THE DISTINCTION: WHY IT IS IMPORTANT

The distinction between active and "non-active" investors is important as it relates to this book. Frequently, I have argued that the Federal government during the last ten years and particularly the last four years, has promoted initiatives and legislation that have definitely and immediately economically benefitted investment bankers, stock brokers and "wealthy active investors" of the world.

Thousands of millions of extra petro dollars, millions of millions of Federal government Q.E. dollars, and sometimes hundreds of millions of stimulus cash (from other "stimulating" central banks of the world) have poured into the American financial markets during the past ten years. The Dow Jones average now regularly establishes new record highs. The rising prices of stocks, bonds, commodities and other financial products have (at least on paper) "potentially" benefitted substantially virtually all current investors in the financial markets.

It is important to understand that substantially all active investors (and stock brokers, investment bankers, etc.) have definitely (not potentially) benefitted economically from these rising prices, frequently on a daily basis as they eagerly buy and sell financial products using Q.E. cash. Regardless of what happens to the Dow Jones average or other world-wide indexes tomorrow, or two months from now, these individuals (including "active investors") have "pocketed" for sure cold hard cash profits, primarily, as the result of Federal government initiatives and Federal Reserve Q.E. stimulation.

On the other hand, the record five-year rise in stock market prices may or may not in the end economically benefit "non-active" passive type investors. For example, a non-active investor who had ten thousand dollars invested in the stock market in early 2009, may have seen the value of that investment (on paper) rise to nearly thirty thousand dollars during the past four years. However, "a repeat" of the financial collapse of 2007/2008 could cause the value of these stock holdings to fall back

below the original ten thousand dollar original investment. Thus, the increased crude oil speculation in the
commodities markets, the "Wall Street bailout", and the
five-year long $3,000,000,000,000 in Q.E. cash, pumped
into the financial markets, could (unlike investment
bankers and wealthy <u>active</u> investors) conceivably in the
end, <u>not</u> economically benefit passive investors at all.

In other words, right now most passive investors
have stocks and bonds that have substantially risen in
value over the last four years. Thus, they have so called
"paper gains" from their stock and bond investments, but
they cannot, of course, put "paper gains" in the bank or
use them to buy a new car, etc.

To potentially take advantage of these price increases that have, in my opinion, been produced by five
years of Federal government handouts and goodies bestowed on the stock and bond markets, such passive investors would have to do what they normally rarely
do. They would have to sell all or part of their stock and
bond investments, while prices are high. They would
then "lock in" bankable profits for themselves.

So called "active investors" do this on a regular basis. Frequently, after a stock market, for example, has
risen by maybe three percent over several days, then the
market in question may fall by perhaps one-half of one
percent on the following day. Media outlets would then
likely report "the market was down slightly today because of "profit taking by traders", or because traders
are "locking in recent gains", etc.

POLITICIANS...AND GENEROUS
ACTIVE INVESTORS

In addition, from a political viewpoint, it is "active" wealthy investors (rather than "passive" investors), as well as high level executives from various investment and commercial banks, that are politically active. It is these individuals and institutions that are most likely to give very large financial donations to campaigns of both political parties, as a means of increasing the financial benefits and other goodies flowing into the financial services sector. Also, it is likely that these same individuals lobby hard for the appointments of "financial services sector friendly" company executives to key federal government positions. Consider the current and recent individuals appointed to serve as Treasury Secretary....most were former higher level executives of investment banking companies.

In the end, the distinction between so-called "active" and "non-active' investors may seem to be overstated, maybe even a diversion from the goal of this book which is most and foremost to dramatically bring down gas prices. Still I have repeatedly put forth the notion that it is various investment bankers, stock brokers and "wealthy active investors" who are, frequently attempting to make a profit by driving up the price of crude oil, knowing that if successful, average working folks are subsequently going to have to pay higher gas prices. In addition I argue that such individuals have sometimes been rewarded for their efforts with Q.E. money from the Federal government, in order to further promote such activities.

I simply want to make clear that it is <u>not</u> all investors and all investment bankers in the financial markets that are creating problems for the middle class. Rather, it is a relatively small group of "specific" active investors, specific investment bankers and brokers, as well as most federal politicians and most Federal Reserve bankers that I am implicating, as frequently causing big problems for the middle class.

CHAPTER EIGHT

THE FINANCIAL SERVICES SECTOR: MIDDLE CLASS SCAPEGOAT?

Based on my observations and discussion in the last chapter and throughout the book, some readers may infer that I am laying all of the economic ills besetting America (and especially the middle class) at the feet of the financial services sector. Some (casual readers) may even feel that I am simply envious or jealous of the rapidly rising financial success of wealthy hedge fund managers, equity fund managers, investment bankers, stock brokers, and other prosperous "active investors". Nothing could be further from the truth. Basic fairness, not envy, is the issue.

I recognize that the financial services sector is a very profitable and very important component of America's overall business sectors. I understand completely that the vast majority of individuals working in the industry are typically good and decent Americans simply trying to make a good living for themselves and their families. Employers and employees within the sector earn, relatively speaking, typically high incomes. Even though investment bankers and their clients frequently have access to "very beneficial" tax rates, still, presumably they contribute significantly to the total federal income taxes collected each year.

So, in a sense, we as Americans all have a small positive stake in the ever-expanding "casino like" business model of exceedingly profitable financial services sector businesses. I want America's financial services sector businesses to be the finest in the world...provided that the "economic playing field" for all businesses in America as a whole is relatively level.

A "TILTED"... UN-LEVEL PLAYING FIELD

If America's economic playing field was genuinely level, then investment bankers, brokers and active wealthy investors could make as much money as possible, while businesses outside the financial services sector, as well as all American families, could compete in a fair environment to better themselves economically. In other words, all businesses and all working individuals would have a "decent shot" in obtaining at least a tiny portion of the sum total of all cash and credit available at any given time in America (or throughout the world).

The problem is, the economic playing field in America is not level. Thanks to the Federal government, it is hugely tilted in favor of investment bankers, brokers and wealthy active investors. One of the reasons I have written this book is to spotlight this unfairness and describe how it has negatively impacted many small business owners outside of the financial services sector (or outside the oil producing sector), as well as economically negatively impacting hundreds of millions of other Americans every day.

CHANGING THE RULES...
IN THE MIDDLE OF THE GAME

In the previous chapter, I briefly mentioned several Federal government initiatives that especially benefit investment bankers and their clients. However, the primary Federal government program that this book has focused upon, of course, is the "gift from heaven" bestowed upon investment bankers and active wealthy investors on December 20, 2000. This legislation, as described, made it easier and safer for investment bankers and wealthy investors to speculate in the crude oil markets. On December 20, 2000, Congress in effect officially changed the rules in the middle of the game.

In so doing, Congress gave up a very adequate system, one used for many years, to determine the price of a barrel of crude oil, which was based on well accepted principles of supply and demand; a system that allowed so called "commercial buyers and commercial sellers" to determine the daily price of a barrel of crude oil. This price was virtually always based on the real, the <u>actual</u>, current availability (or the <u>actual</u> potential future availability) of crude oil at the time of crude oil purchases (similar to my experience, over the years, purchasing peace lilies in Florida).

Instead, as repeated often, when Congress gave up the established system in December of 2000, they in effect promoted conditions that created a new way to determine crude oil and other commodity prices. The new system gave speculators the seemingly absurd right to "safely" enter almost any energy commodities market and "bet" simply on whether the price of the commodity would eventually rise or fall. This, as explained earlier, allowed for the very real potential that these "betters" could actually "force up" the price of a commodity like crude oil. Higher crude oil prices eventually result in higher prices for fuel.

Over the past 12 years, such commodity speculation has been hugely profitable to many investment bankers, stock brokers, hedge fund managers, active wealthy investors, oil company executives, oil company stock holders and wealthy oil well owners. On the other hand, the financial advantages derived by these individuals, have at the same time directly created financial disadvantages for tens of millions of Americans and millions of small business owners, as the result of artificially high fuel prices.

So, clearly understand the issue at hand. It is not simply that the Federal government during the past 12 years has bestowed extra goodies upon a wealthy, politically influential business sector. No, the problem goes beyond that. Such investment bankers and other wealthy individuals, who are able to vote and donate substantial amounts of cash to re-election campaigns, have probably always received "special attention" from politicians. Most of us in the middle class small business community recognize and accept this fact. We are not necessarily complaining about the Federal government making it easier for large politically connected companies and individuals to make even more money…unless, of course, the increased profitability of such large companies <u>directly</u> causes decreases in the profitability of small businesses throughout America.

My contention, as often described, is just that. The use of these (Congressionally bestowed) goodies has led to artificially high and unstable fuel prices that have hugely benefitted two business sectors, while at the same time (for over ten years) have negatively impacted middle class small business owners and has depleted disposable income of tens of millions of middle class families. These individuals have been forced to accept an ever smaller portion of America's "economic pie of disposable income". (As described in the previous chapter, such widespread decreases of middle class disposable income are "job vaporizers".)

A MORE LEVEL PLAYING FIELD: THE PATH NOT TAKEN

"Out of control speculation", especially in the crude oil futures market has led, during the past 12 years, to a <u>massive</u> transfer of wealth (in the form of petro dollars) from less prosperous and middle class Americans directly into the bank accounts of companies and individuals within the financial services sector and the crude oil production sector.

So again, my position as described repeatedly is clear. "The enhanced right to speculate" was gained illegitimately, is anti-capitalistic, does not promote the "greater good" within America and flies directly into the face of rote common sense.

143

Thus, the "right to speculate" should be revoked, overturned, banned or whatever, by the Federal government…the sooner, the better. Banning crude oil speculation would be a large first step in the process of "leveling America's economic playing field" for all businesses.

DECEMBER 20, 2000: WHAT WERE THEY THINKING?

So legislation passed on December 20, 2000, provided the heavy duty earth moving machinery that eventually produced an increasingly un-level economic playing field in America. The legislation was overwhelmingly approved by both Democrats and Republicans and signed into law by President Clinton. It is quite possible that many of these legislators did not fully realize that the Bill's passage in December, 2000, would eventually lead to a doubling, then tripling, then quadrupling of crude oil prices and of course, much higher gas prices.

With Republicans controlling Congress, an "increasingly" pro-business Bill Clinton as President, and a "lame duck" session of Congress in progress, the mood of the day was to bring "finality" to the years of efforts to promote government deregulation of the financial markets. Another hugely significant deregulation type bill known as the Financial Modernization Act of 1999, had been passed into law the year before. This Act in effect, finally overturned the Glass Steagall Act, which had placed significant regulatory restrictions on the financial services sector.

The Glass Steagall Act originated as a response to the actions of commercial bankers, investment bankers and brokers before and during the Great Depression. (It is however, interesting that the mood toward deregulating the financial markets was still in high gear in December of 2000, even though the NASDAQ stock index had crashed, losing almost half of its value, due to a "bursting bubble" during the year 2000. As I have often alluded to, the monetary and political influence of the financial services sector simply cannot be overestimated.)

BENEFIT OF THE DOUBT: REFUSING TO CORRECT THE PROBLEM

If Congressional legislators had made an honest mistake on December 20, 2000, then it stands to reason that as gas prices eventually began to rise rapidly, a few years into this century, then these legislators would have taken <u>serious</u> steps to deal with the problem. In other words, Congressional members could have said: "Whoa, wait a minute! We had almost 20 years of relatively low and stable gas prices during most of the 80's and virtually all of the 90's, and now the price of crude oil (and gasoline) has more than tripled in price. Since passage of the December 20, 2000 Legislation, huge increases in crude oil speculation have occurred. Gee, I wonder if these incredible increases in crude oil speculation in recent years, are causing higher crude oil prices, followed by higher fuel prices. Maybe we made a mistake. Come, let us gather together quickly and debate the issue of speculation, and perhaps revoke the provisions of this legislation that have promoted runaway speculation in the crude oil markets. Or better still, we could simply pass new legislation that supersedes the December 20, 2000 legislation and would criminally ban crude oil speculation."

PROTECTING SPECULATION...AND
IGNORING HIGH GAS PRICES

Unfortunately, the Federal government has done virtually nothing of real significance to determine if "speculation" is causing higher and less stable crude oil prices. In fact, I think it is fair to say that federal policy makers have actually protected speculation during the past twelve years by, for the most part, simply "ignoring" the potential "common sense" solution that I have outlined in this book for bringing down crude oil prices very quickly (that would be a complete ban on crude oil speculation, at least temporarily.).

Of course, when gas prices exceed $4.00 per gallon, in many areas of the country, then policy makers are forced to answer a few questions regarding high crude oil prices and/or crude oil speculation. As described, such policy makers simply then refer the problem to the Commodity Futures Trading Commission. Again, as described earlier, this "slow motion agency" has been unusually ineffective in controlling crude oil speculation.

So I stand by my assertion that most federal politicians are beholden to the politically powerful financial services sector and oil producing sector. Unfortunately, most Americans are unaware of the magnitude of this favoritism...but the plot thickens.

THE Q.E. PROGRAMS: ADDING INSULT TO INJURY

So here is a quick review: First, Congress produced the dubious right to "safely speculate" in the Crude Oil Commodities Market back in December of 2000. Secondly, during the past 13 years the Federal government has protected this dubious right by refusing to take away or seriously restrict use of "the right to speculate". Thus, we in America and others worldwide continue to deal with artificially high and unstable fuel prices...but it gets worse.

Thirdly, the U.S. Federal Government is currently, and has been for the previous five years, actively providing the equivalent of "cold cash" for investment bankers and wealthy active investors from all over the world to actually purchase additional crude oil futures contracts, swap contracts, etc. (Also, in recent years, other countries and their Central Banks have begun adopting policies that "bail out" investors or otherwise pump additional cash into financial services sectors "to stimulate economies" or "devalue currencies".) This extra government cash has almost without question driven up the price of crude oil and gasoline during the last five years. The only question is...how great is the inflationary impact?

Currently, the Federal Reserve stands willing to purchase up to 85 billion dollars of debt instruments each month from the so called primary dealers. In other words, the equivalent of a million dollars of cold cash is being pumped 85,000 different times into one business sector each month, in order that the sector's businesses and wealthy active clients will have extra money to bet (that is invest) as they see fit.

I am sure that bankers at the Federal Reserve would prefer that stock brokers and other active investors use the Q.E. cash to simply purchase stock in a wide array of American companies. Nevertheless, policy makers know that an extra 85 billion Q.E. dollars a month in the hands of investors will almost certainly increase additional purchases of various commodities including crude oil. This potential additional "government sponsored" increase in demand for crude oil can cause increases in the price of crude oil…which then leads to higher fuel prices.

Various economists during the past few years have opposed the Q.E. programs, especially the more recent Q.E. programs, because of (among other reasons) their potential to inflate the ever changing prices of various essential commodities, including crude oil.

So the ugly picture is now complete. The last pieces of the puzzle have been put in place. America's Federal government produced the right "to more easily and safely speculate", it has protected the right for more than 13 years and finally, during the past five years, has promoted the use of the right (to speculate), by using the Federal Reserve to dole out "Q.E. cold cash" to investment bankers and wealthy active investors.

HIGH GAS PRICES AND Q.E. GOODIES:
A GRAND CONSPIRACY THEORY?

So, am I suggesting that powerful Congressional leaders, Treasury Secretaries, Federal Reserve bankers, wealthy private equity fund managers, wealthy hedge fund managers, oil company executives, etc. all met behind closed doors in the middle of the night and concocted a "grand scheme" to raise crude oil prices, to be followed by increases in fuel prices? The "scheme" would, in effect, economically shaft most middle class and less prosperous Americans, while hugely benefitting oil producers and the investment banking community.

Did many of these same individuals meet seven or eight years later and decide that "the time was ripe" to initiate the Q.E. Programs? Did they correctly conclude that such programs would hugely benefit investment bankers and active investors as the price of stocks, commodities and other financial products rose in price and popularity, while once again "shafting" most of middle class America as a result of even higher prices for gasoline and other essential goods?

My answer is "no", with regard to the possibility of highly organized secretive type meetings described above. Actually, it is impossible to know exactly what went on before and during passage of the Commodities Modernization Act back in December of 2000. Ditto 2008 before the Q.E. programs were initiated. Even today it is impossible to know exactly what Federal policy makers and those lobbying on behalf of the financial services sector and the oil industry are thinking.

What is possible to know is the Federal government's actual response during the past twelve years to rapidly rising or artificially high fuel prices. As I have described, there has been no effective government response, just excuses. In fact, the Federal government using the Federal Reserve, has made matters worse during the past four years by providing extra cash for crude oil speculators to potentially bid up the price of crude oil (which then causes fuel prices to rise).

CRITICIZING THIS BOOK: A GOOD THING

In the days ahead, my biggest concern is that this book will remain "unread" or otherwise ignored. To the extent that the book eventually receives substantial criticism or negative reaction, then that would be a "good thing"…a great thing. The book will have received a degree of publicity (presumably the book will have advocates as well).

Most critics of the book will have read the book thoroughly and have legitimate concerns and complaints. Other critics, however, may have "half-read" the book with the simple objective of developing negative "sound bites" and other critical hyperbole for the benefit of their clients, readers, viewers or listeners. Their objective might be, in essence, to discourage members of their audiences from actually reading and evaluating the book for themselves. For the benefit of these particular critics, I have specifically included the five following "clarifications".

AM I PROMOTING…CLASS WARFARE?

(1) Some critics may claim that the book promotes the notion that wealthy Americans are taking advantage of less prosperous, middle class type citizens.

MY RESPONSE: Nowhere in this book do I claim that prosperous and wealthier individuals as a group have caused economic hardships for less prosperous and middle class individuals. My argument is that a relatively small group of individuals, typically wealthier, and working in an around the financial services sector, have created problems for most Americans, including the middle class.

Such individuals include various investment bankers, brokers and other active investors like hedge fund managers and private equity fund managers that regularly "bet heavily" in the commodities markets, including the crude oil markets. Other such wealthier individuals include "non-competing" oil company executive types, as well as actual owners of multiple oil wells. "Rounding out" this book's informal list of potential culprits, would be various typically prosperous Congressional members, Treasury Secretaries, Regulatory Agency members, Presidents, and some Federal Reserve bankers.

In particular, this incredibly small group of government employees, as explained repeatedly, have produced, protected, and promoted "runaway speculation" in the crude oil markets, which can inflate gasoline prices. Higher prices for fuel (and other commodities that are necessities) economically hurt most all Americans, but less prosperous and middle class families are disproportionately negatively impacted because of their shortages of disposable income.

AM I PROMOTING...
GOVERNMENT HANDOUTS?

(2) Other critics may argue that this book demands Federal government handouts for less prosperous and middle class Americans.

MY RESPONSE: Nowhere in this book do I demand Federal government "handouts" to less prosperous or middle class Americans. Rather, I argue for the need of Federal government initiatives that potentially increase the disposable income of (typically hard pressed) middle income Americans. The book's plan to bring down gas prices is an example of such a Federal government initiative. Also, I argue that if the Federal government sees fit to use the Federal Reserve "to create" two or three trillion dollars in order "to stimulate" one business sector, the financial services sector, then the Federal government should consider using some of that money to quickly stimulate individuals other than investment bankers, brokers and other active investors.

AM I PROMOTING...
TAX INCREASES FOR THE WEALTHY?

(3) In addition, critics may argue that this book promotes "give backs" from prosperous and wealthy individuals.

<u>MY</u> <u>RESPONSE:</u>   Nowhere in this book do I call for "give backs" from the group of Americans considered to be prosperous or wealthy. For example, nowhere in the book do I call for tax increases on more prosperous or wealthy individuals. I do, very briefly, describe how investment bankers, brokers and active investors make frequent use of certain classes of income and favorable rates of taxation. However, I do <u>not</u> call for any changes in these classifications or changes in tax rates.

AM I PROMOTING…SOCIALISM?

(4) Some critics may even argue that the book promotes "Socialism" because the book promotes Federal government intervention into the affairs of private businesses.

<u>MY</u> <u>RESPONSE:</u> Countries that have adopted a Socialistic framework for governance, frequently own some of the largest companies located in the country. They also typically promote a high level of government regulation for the majority of larger corporations.

In this book, rather than promote Socialism, surely I have made clear my admiration and support for "competition driven" free market capitalism (roughly speaking, the opposite of Socialism). In my opinion, the problem with government run businesses (or agencies for that matter) is that "the possibility of economic gain <u>or</u> economic loss" does not play a major role in everyday decision making. Thus, government run businesses are almost always going to be less efficient than "true" capitalistic type businesses.

In this book, <u>nowhere</u> have I supported a government takeover of businesses or more federal regulation of all private businesses. Instead I have argued that the Federal government should confront executives of businesses in <u>two</u> sectors, the financial services sector and the crude oil producing sector.

Ironically, intervention is needed because the Federal government itself has bestowed "special goodies" and other benefits unto these politically powerful and wonderfully generous business sectors. Now, I argue that we the people need to force Federal government officials (not so much to regulate) but to constrain or take back some of these "illegitimate goodies" for the benefit of smaller and less politically connected middle class small business owners and families (as described in previous chapters.) Simply put, I argue; (1) that crude oil speculation should be banned; (2) that oil producing companies be forced to compete and; (3) that Q.E. trillion dollar stimulants/giveaways be reconsidered. That's all.

AM I ENVIOUS...OF OTHERS?

(5) Finally, some critics may argue that since I am still firmly entrenched in the middle class, after owning businesses for 32 years, that somehow the mission of this book reflects my envy or bitterness toward more successful business owners or individuals.

<u>MY</u> <u>RESPONSE</u>: This criticism, if used, would be frivolous and unjustified indeed. As I mentioned earlier, the businesses that my wife and I owned and ran for 32

years were, generally speaking, only marginally profitable year after year. We typically did not pay a lot of income taxes, but we paid "a ton" of payroll taxes, which are Social Security and Medicare taxes (small business owners with employees have to personally "match" the payroll taxes paid by their employees). Then at the end of the year, the small business owner, as a sole proprietor, has to pay "double" payroll taxes....15.3% of his business income.

So, in the end we paid out a goodly amount to the IRS in payroll taxes, to employees for wages, to landlords for rent, to suppliers for wholesale merchandise, and to local governments for business licenses, property taxes, etc. However, always enough money was left over to pay our personal bills, raise a family, see both children graduate from college/medical school, etc.

We, of course, hoped for higher profits each year; not necessarily to buy "more personal stuff" or to receive more accolades as "successful business owners". Rather, increased business profitability to us meant a chance to take more "time off" from the businesses. My guess is that most small business owners view "success" in a similar manner.

Like most business owners, our claim would be that we provided unusually high value products and service to our customers. Beyond that, we would argue that ours was a business with a heart. My wife, in particular has a gift for encouraging and uplifting others. For over 32 years she had ample opportunity to do just that. Success, of course, is not always measured in economic terms.

With regard to other truly successful business owners and successful, prosperous or wealthy individuals, I wish them well. I truly admire any individual who has honestly and without the aid of government assistance or favoritism, become economically prosperous. I hope such individuals become even more prosperous in the days ahead.

Of course, my feelings do not really matter. What is important for the reader to understand is that many individuals who make a ton of money each year for themselves are also generating revenue that produces many, many jobs...down the line. In addition, such individuals are hugely responsible for creating products, services, or entertainment that improve our quality of life. Consider the contributions of typically more prosperous individuals like doctors, dentists, veterinarians, actors, actresses, great athletes and successful business owners.

A good example would be the late Steve Jobs. His unique talents and determination allowed his company to produce products that are the envy of the world. His company provided or produced, directly and indirectly, millions of jobs throughout America and the world. In addition, he and many other high tech innovators have produced a breathtaking array of sophisticated products. (I am someone who does not clearly understand how to hold a typical camera. Yet, using my iPhone, I can now easily take videos of my grandchildren and send them to other individuals hundreds of miles away.)

Thus, I do not understand how any "right thinking" individual could claim that Steve Jobs made too much money each year before his passing; or claim that his family is currently accumulating too much wealth. Of course, it has to be noted, and goes without saying, that the number of jobs produced and the unique products/services created, vary greatly from one wealthy individual to another.

THE FINANCIAL SERVICES SECTOR: CONCLUDING REMARKS

I began this chapter by stating that I would like to see America's financial sector be the best in the world. I stand by that statement, with this caveat. The financial services sector should be able to maintain or reach this goal with substantially less help from the Federal government. For now, I am not seriously challenging all of the various government policies or initiatives that I think unfairly benefit investment bankers and prosperous investors actively trading in the financial markets.

For example, I have not discussed or even mentioned the fact that six years ago the Federal government essentially abandoned a long standing "informal" government policy regarding "reckless risk taking" by investment companies, which was frequently referred to as "moral hazard". The policy demanded that the federal government not "bailout" such investment companies, because to do so, would….dah…in fact "encourage" reckless betting by such companies. (Actually, I think the phrase "moral hazard" may have been officially deleted from the American Lexicon.)

Similarly, no mention in this book has been made of the Federal, State and industry regulators "looking the other way", while lenders and investment bankers perfected a business model in the years leading up to the financial collapse of 2007 and 2008. The business model was callously referred to within the industry as "you'll be gone…I'll be gone".

In other words commercial bankers and lenders who were making dubious loans without verifying income or without using traditional income/debt ratios to qualify such loans, would "be gone". The investment bankers who rapidly purchased these dubious loans, bundled them into "a company", sold bonds from "the company", and then sometimes used credit default swaps to bet on the bonds…well they too would "be gone" when the proverbial "do-do" hit the fan months later. The use of this business model resulted in many tens of millions of American homes being stripped of all equity.

Finally, I have ignored the fact that federal policy makers and "regulators of all stripes" continue to allow the world's "big betters"….that is, active investors, investment bankers and brokers to engage in the practice of "referencing" (as opposed to the legitimate practice of "insuring") various bond purchases when using credit default swaps type financial instruments. Such "referencing" is a way of betting that a particular batch of bonds will "go bad"…without actually having to purchase the bonds in question. Ironically, it is the investment company or insurance company, who takes such "referenced" bets, that puts financial sectors of the world at risk…think $148 billion to bailout AIG in 2007 and

2008 or more recently, in 2012, consider the $6 billion loss attributed to the "London Whale". (In my opinion, it was (1) the use of credit default swaps to "reference" bond issuances and (2) the "I'll be gone…you'll be gone" business model, that were the primary reasons for the financial collapse of 2007 and 2008.)

Instead of focusing on such issues as the three illustrations just described, I am instead only directly challenging the Federal government's production, protection and promotion of "runaway speculation" in the crude oil markets. Such policies represent an active role by the Federal government in promoting (not lowering) high gas prices; an active role by the Federal government in decreasing (not increasing) the disposable income of middle class families.

At this time I am not particularly interested in further discussing the financial services sector. The mission of this book is first and foremost to encourage the Federal government to help bring down gas prices. A second mission is to illustrate how such government initiatives that directly and quickly promote widespread increases in disposable income, could in turn generate a massive economic recovery. Further discussions concerning "Wall Street" could conceivably confuse the real mission of this book.

Nevertheless, I have no choice but to further discuss the various Q.E. programs initiated during the last five years, because they have, as described, directly promoted even higher gas and diesel fuel prices and have thus negatively impacted most middle class citizens. In addition, the latest round of "Quantitative Easing" (Q.E.4) is "open ended", meaning the monthly injections of "crude oil buying cash" could possibly continue for months or years.

HOW MUCH IS...ONE BILLION/ONE TRILLION DOLLARS?

In the next chapter, which focuses on the Federal government's Q.E. programs, the terms "billions" and "trillions" of dollars will be frequently mentioned. So this is probably a good point in the book to inject a short section regarding terminology; in particular, regarding the terms "billions" and "trillions"; or even more specifically, the phrases "billions of dollars" or "trillions of dollars".

It is my belief that one of the many reasons that middle class America is and has been in such financial duress during the past five to ten years, is the general lack of understanding about just exactly how much money is involved when, for example, a politician or banker is talking about 20 billion dollars here or 4 trillion dollars there, etc.

We all know the value of one thousand dollars, five hundred thousand dollars or nine hundred thousand dollars. Most of us realize that one million dollars is a little more than $999,000. More precisely, one million dollars spent is one thousand dollars spent one thousand times.

ONE MILLION DOLLARS: I GET IT!

So, most adult citizens clearly understand the value of one million dollars. However, how many citizens clearly understand the monetary value of "one billion" dollars? How about "one trillion" dollars?   Since the word "million" is better conceptualized than the word "billion" or "trillion", I have and will, during the course of this book, frequently use million dollar equivalents either parenthetically or to replace the terms "billions" or "trillions". Conceptualizing the true value of one trillion dollars is a little like trying to get "your brain around" the actual distance in miles between planet Earth and planet Jupiter.

For the record, one billion dollars spent is one million dollars spent, one thousand times. One trillion dollars spent is one million dollars spent, one million times. In other words, one billion is equivalent to 1,000 million; one trillion is equivalent to "one million times a million".

Considered yet another way; one billion is equivalent to 1,000 X 1,000,000 equals 1,000,000,000 (or one billion).   One trillion is equivalent to 1,000,000 X 1,000,000 = 1,000,000,000,000 (or one trillion).

To better explain my decision regarding terminology, consider several examples. During 2008 and 2009, two different Presidents, two different Treasury Secretaries and a few "top guns" at the Federal Reserve Bank decided to provide one company, AIG, Inc., 148 billion dollars in cash and credit. After hearing of such a bailout, most citizens likely complained and perhaps noted that the large sum of money was just another favor for one of Wall Street's "special companies." Unfortunately, within a few days, most Americans likely forgot the exact amount of money actually involved, etc.

However, if the Federal government or various media outlets had broken down this amount of money into "millions of dollars", then the outcry might have been more intense and lasted longer. Many ordinary citizens would have complained, that the Federal government had not justified its case for providing one company that much money. Subsequently, many citizens might have demanded that more information be provided by the government before such a large amount of money was doled out.

In other words, which phrase is more meaningful? Which phrase gives you a better picture of how much money is actually involved? (1) "AIG received roughly 148 billion dollars in federal government bailout funds" or the phrase (2) "AIG received the equivalent of one million dollars, one hundred and forty eight thousand different times from the federal government"?

Similarly, and even more importantly, the Federal Reserve Bank during the last five years has initiated four separate programs, known as Q.E. programs. Mostly, as a result of these Q.E. programs, the Federal Reserve Bank has pumped more than three trillion dollars into the financial services sector. Under the current Q.E. program, the Federal Reserve is pumping 85 billion dollars into the financial services sector each month. This eighty five billion dollar monthly figure may or may not arouse concern amongst the citizenry. However, what if the Federal Reserve had announced or the media had actually reported that the new Q.E. program would involve the Federal Reserve, in effect, pumping one million dollars of cold cash into the financial services sector, eighty five thousand times each month…for an extended period of time. (Gee, think of the time required for you personally to write out a check for one million dollars, 148,000 different times).

Or… how about the federal deficit? During the past five years the Federal government has spent each year roughly one trillion dollars more than the actual tax revenues that it has received for the year. The yearly federal deficits could have been described this way. During each of the past five years the Federal government has spent "roughly" one million dollars, one million times (during the year), in excess of incoming tax revenues. In other words, the Federal government last year spent (more than) $1,000,000, one million times…that it did not "really have on hand" (as the result of tax revenues) to spend.

CHAPTER NINE

Q.E. MONEY: THE DEAD ELEPHANT IN THE ROOM

To me, the four different Q.E. programs initiated during the past four years, are extremely controversial and not clearly understood by perhaps 98% of American citizens. Q.E. stands for Quantitative Easing. The very phrase describing the programs suggests the possibility of "a hustle" of some sort.

During the past five years, the Federal Reserve Bank of the United States has used four Q.E. programs to, in effect, pump roughly $3,000,000,000,000.000 (that would be 3 trillion dollars) into the financial services sector. The third Q.E. program is a little different from the other three Q.E. programs. It is sometimes referred to as "twisted Q.E.". As noted, the four programs were initiated and carried out by the Federal Reserve Bank, but almost certainly have "had the blessing" of high level policy makers in the Executive Branch of the Federal government.

The stated goals of producing such "magic money", is to keep interest rates low, stimulate the economy and thus produce more jobs. Obviously, the financial markets are stimulated and "stock broker type" jobs are created. However, the obvious question in my mind is whether or not such monetary stimulation of America's

"Wall Streets", also produces <u>significant</u> increases in middle class type jobs on America's main streets.

Seemingly, the primary objections (mostly by Republican Congressional members) to the programs, are not related to their middle class job producing capacity, but rather the objections focus on the possibility that the Q.E. programs will cause increased inflation rates. One of the stated goals of the Q.E. programs is after all to increase the supply of money. (Actually, the Treasury Department creates the currency used. The Fed then buys and subsequently issues the currency.)

The inflation rate, which is typically based on the consumer price index, has remained relatively low during the last five years. Thus, at this point, serious, hard-nosed ongoing opposition to the Q.E. programs by either political party is relatively absent.

Nevertheless, my view is this. When 19 bankers, none of whom are elected by the tax payers, get together regularly and decide to pump over 3 trillion dollars of "magic money" into <u>one</u> business sector over a period of five years (with no specific end in sight), that is controversial. I have stated my primary objection to the Q.E. programs in the previous chapter....stimulus money from the Q.E. programs is being used to bid up crude oil prices resulting in higher gas prices. However, I have other serious questions about the Q.E. programs and their impact on middle class America that I will detail shortly.

THE FEDERAL RESERVE SYSTEM: THE BASICS

The Federal Reserve System is frequently referred to as The Federal Reserve or simply "the Fed". It was created by Congress a 100 years ago and is the Central Banking System of the United States. The Federal Reserve System is headed by seven individuals (referred to as Governors) that are appointed by the President and approved by Congress. They make up the Federal Reserve Board, headed by a Reserve Board Chairman.

Presidents of the 12 regional Federal Reserve Banks join with the seven (appointed) Federal Reserve Governors and together debate and decide upon key policy decisions. This important group of (unelected) individuals forms the Federal Open Market Committee (FOMC). The FOMC meets regularly to discuss, to debate and ultimately to vote on various policy initiatives such as the Q.E. programs.

The Federal Reserve System serves many roles and has many relatively uncontroversial responsibilities. For example, just as you and I have a bank into which we make deposits and upon which we write checks, the U.S. Government; that is, the Treasury Department uses the Federal Reserve Bank for the same purposes. Always, the Federal Reserve is required to guard against the possibility of "bank runs" or other bank instability.

The three main policy objectives of the Federal Reserve are to promote employment, prevent unhealthy inflation (or deflation), and to influence interest rates. The Federal Reserve's role could be described as stimulating the economy without creating excess inflation. Until the financial collapse in 2007 and 2008, the FOMC or the Federal Reserve accomplished these goals by using its "tools" to promote increases or decreases in the prevailing short term and long term interest rates. For example, promoting higher interest rates typically slows down the American economy and decreases the chances for higher inflation. On the other hand, promoting the reduction of interest rates historically has stimulated the economy.

In this regard, it has been widely accepted that the Federal Reserve should have a good deal of independence in deciding the appropriate direction of interest rates. That is, the Federal Reserve Governors and Bankers, being the "impartial experts", should be relatively free from undue influence from Republicans and Democrats when it comes to influencing the direction of interest rates. (Even though the Federal Reserve System, a public/private institution, enjoys a substantial amount of independence, little doubt exists that Congress and especially the President exercise some degree of influence over the actions of Federal Reserve top officials. After all, the President appoints and Congress must approve board members, and Congress sets the salaries of many high-level Federal Reserve bankers.)

The financial collapse in 2007 and 2008 and the subsequent bailout of many financial institutions has seriously impacted the Federal Reserve. During the financial crisis, the Federal Reserve used its tools to reduce short term interest rates to almost zero and longer term interest rates to record lows. Thus, the traditional tools that the Fed had used over the years to stimulate the economy (by forcing down interest rates) had in effect been used up. Thus, during the past five years, the Federal Reserve has embarked on policies that have never before been used on such a scale in the United States, in attempts to stimulate the economy. Examples would be the Q.E. programs and various pledges to keep interest rates near zero for years into the future.

So the Federal Reserve has, in a very real sense, entered an entirely new era during the last five years. Hard questions are long overdue....unless, of course, taxpayers in the end do not mind potentially providing million dollar gifts to investment bankers and wealthy active investors, worldwide.

FEDERAL RESERVE BANKERS: DEFEND THYSELF

Given the fact that none of the decision makers comprising the FOMC are actually "chosen by the electorate" and given the amount of dollars being pumped into the economy during the last five years, I think the members of the Federal Reserve's Open Market Committee should be required to better publicize and defend their monetary strategy used during the past five years, to the American people. (Remember it was the FOMC that failed to adequately anticipate the financial collapse of 2007 and 2008).

My suggestion would be a mandatory twenty to thirty hours of public hearings carried live nationwide on prime time radio and television over a period of two or three days...remember we are talking about the creation of $85 billion (or 85,000 million dollars) each month. The proposed conference could be a one-time occurrence, an annual "get together", or maybe a once every four years, well publicized meeting.

Present at the proposed hearings would be all members of the FOMC, the U.S. President and leaders of both parties of Congress, together with economists that favor and oppose the Q.E. programs. When this potential hearing concludes, perhaps Federal Reserve bankers and their defenders can successfully make their case for the legitimacy and need for the Q.E. programs. However, an important aspect of such hearings is that economic experts will be present that are qualified to challenge Federal Reserve bankers, regarding the Q.E. programs.

I understand that most Americans are not particularly interested in learning more about the Q.E. programs. They are busy trying to "make ends meet", raising families, etc. Still, millions of us would like to know, in simple and straightforward language, much more about the rationale and implications of the Q.E. programs.

I also understand that it is seemingly absurd for a mere citizen, like myself, to suggest that a powerful institution like the Federal Reserve should, actually very publicly, defend its recent policy decisions. But what am I to do? By the end of 2013, potentially over

$3,000,000,000,000 (3 trillion dollars) will have been created with relatively few questions asked by powerful politicians and influential media types.

Furthermore, I understand that the Federal Reserve, as noted, is at least semi-independent. Beyond that, high level Federal Reserve officials make decisions and take other independent actions that are frequently considered to be "private". The Governmental Accounting Office (the GAO) is allowed to audit some practices of the Federal Reserve, while many others are "off limits". Many Federal Reserve bankers place a high value on this "right to secrecy". They will, no doubt, resist, perhaps even refuse my call for more openness, more answers to tough questions.

The "right to secrecy" in government operations is sometimes warranted. For example, neither I nor most other Americans are demanding that the CIA divulge its "secret operations". I am not even particularly interested in the "secret considerations" of the FOMC, back when these decisions primarily affected the direction of interest rates.

I am not necessarily calling for an end to the Federal Reserve's long standing independent, semi-independent or public/private status. I am simply arguing that the Federal Reserve is now engaged in controversial activities that are historic in nature. Again they are in effect currently creating 85,000 million dollars each month that is primarily used by one business sector and its clients. Thus, Federal Reserve bankers, at least this one time, should be willing to justify their actions for the benefit of tens of millions of taxpaying citizens.

The deliberations of the FOMC are, of course, not completely secretive. The transcripts from the Central Bank's meetings are eventually made available after five years. In addition, the Federal Reserve Chairman typically answers questions on a regular basis from Congressional committee members. Still, a more public, wide ranging debate over the Q.E. programs is currently warranted.

THE GRAND CONFERENCE: OBVIOUS AND NOT SO OBVIOUS TOPICS

Should a conference ever be convened to discuss the positives and the negatives of the Q.E. programs, Federal Reserve bankers and their defenders will no doubt justify the programs for at least seven reasons. I will list these seven reasons and briefly respond to each reason.

However, I am most interested to hear the comments of Federal Reserve bankers regarding two topics that have received relatively little publicity during the last five years. The first topic revolves around the accuracy and durability of the figure that the Federal Reserve reports regularly as its inventory (of debt instruments, etc.). During the last five years this figure has risen from less than one trillion dollars to approximately three trillion dollars at the end of 2012 and will likely pass the four trillion dollar mark by the end of 2013. If this approximately four trillion dollar figure is overstated, or if the current figure is subject to future significant declines (under various situations), then potentially huge financial losses are possible.

The second topic revolves around the issue of fairness, which I have substantially discussed during the last two chapters. In particular, I have complained that the Q.E. programs have hugely benefitted the "Wall Streets of the World", while offering very few concrete, immediate benefits to most middle class Americans.

Experts may have additional points of interest to discuss at the proposed conference. I am, for sure, not an expert on the Federal Reserve or the Q.E. programs. I am simply an individual with many years of business experience. Using this experience, I may see potential problems that are not being adequately publicized and discussed. For example, like any business owner, I understand the potential "hidden" dangers of a "rapidly rising" business inventory figure. In the case of the Q.E. programs, thousands of millions of dollars (potentially millions of millions of dollars) could be at stake.

I am genuinely looking forward to some unique "food for thought" from bankers at the proposed "Grand Conference". My complaints during the last two chapters make it clear that, at this time, I think the four Q.E. programs, particularly the last three, were bad economic policy. However, participants at the conference could change my opinion. I am always willing to reduce, momentarily, my most strongly held beliefs to mere assumptions, as I listen to, read about, or consider unique ideas or new information. (Such an approach, I believe, may be pretty much the only way to avoid being "hustled" on a regular basis.)

IN DEFENSE OF Q.E: THE WELL WORN BASIC ARGUMENTS

The defenders of the 4 Q.E. programs will surely put forth the following seven justifications for the programs. I will add my thoughts after each justification.

1. **FEDERAL RESERVE BANKERS:** We, at the Federal Reserve have been able to greatly expand the money supply and thus stimulate the economy and create jobs during the last four years, without producing significant increases in yearly inflation.

MY RESPONSE: True, the Federal Reserve, as described earlier, has been able to create over $3,000,000,000,000 (3 trillion) in extra money without creating significant inflation, as measured by the traditional "consumer price index". The very big unanswered question is this: Are the Fed Q.E. programs creating "substantially unrecognized inflation in the financial markets?"

Also, it is important to understand that when Goldman Sachs, for example, receives one million dollars of Q.E. money, then brokers at the company can in effect use the money as collateral and purchase perhaps ten million dollars of crude oil contracts (that is, ten percent down and 90% on credit). Thus, the monthly "stimulating effect" (or the inflationary impact) of the current

Q.E. programs, it seems to me, is potentially far greater than the $85,000,000,000 in monthly Q.E. purchases.

I have already complained that the Q.E. programs have inflated the prices of various essential commodities, such as crude oil. However, gauging inflationary pressures overall, inside the financial markets, is more difficult.

Since the Federal Reserve (using "primary dealers") purchases mortgage backed securities and other debt instruments from bankers and wealthy active investors across America and worldwide, the vast majority of the Q.E. money stays within the American and worldwide financial markets. This could account for the lack of inflation among the "common folk" (as measured by the CPI), despite roughly three trillion dollars in extra cash being issued during the last five years.

Similarly, are the Q.E. dollars also increasing the purchase of risky bonds and subsequently increasing the number of credit default swaps that are being bought and sold which insure or "reference" such risky bonds? In short, is the approximately three trillion dollars in Q.E. cash during the last five years, helping to inflate a bubble within the financial markets similar to the one that "popped' back in 2007?

My thoughts regarding the Fed's claim of Q.E. job creation are these. Pumping one million dollars, three million times into one already prosperous business sector over a period of five years is going to create some new jobs. As I have previously argued, most of these jobs will be well paying "stock broker" type jobs. Obviously, additional employees will be needed to handle three trillion in additional betting...I mean, buying and selling of financial products in the financial markets. My complaint is again, that the Q.E. programs have not created enough widespread middle class employment opportunities, either as immediate or "trickle down" effects of the programs.

At the conference, Federal Reserve bankers will probably argue that they are ill equipped to stimulate or produce quick economic benefits for Jack's Hardware Store or Karen's Midtown Diner (located many miles from "the financial district"). Partly because of this potential excuse, I have suggested that the President and Congressional leaders from both Parties also attend the proposed Grand Q.E. Conference.

In a highly publicized and heavily viewed forum, these politicians and bankers would be in a position to do, "what they all claim they want to do"; that is, to help middle class families and uh don't forget...middle class small business owners. So, here, in front of the lights and microphones, is their chance.

The question to be answered is this. What can you pledge to do that would increase disposable income for tens of millions of middle class families in a way and magnitude, similar to the immediate and definite economic help that the Q.E. programs have provided to investment bankers and wealthy active investors...hint, hint: For starters, ban crude oil speculation, force oil companies to compete, and reevaluate the Q.E. programs with regard to the "fairness factor".

2. **FEDERAL RESERVE BANKERS:** Bankers will argue that the Q.E. program have kept long term interest rates low during the last five years. Thus, with lower mortgage rates, more homes have been bought, sold or refinanced.

MY RESPONSE: It is, I believe, hard to know for sure if the Q.E. programs were actually needed to keep mortgage rates low. When the programs were initiated, such longer term interest rates were at record lows and typically falling.

At any rate, many tens of millions of middle class Americans have, during the past seven years, lost the home equity required or credit needed to take advantage of these lower mortgage rates. The low mortgage rates are, of course, an economic benefit to more prosperous or wealthy individuals who have ample credit, equity, or disposable income to purchase a house (or maybe several houses). Even so, if these individuals currently own a home they will likely have to accept a depressed price for the home they are presumably selling.

3. **FEDERAL RESERVE BANKERS:** Bankers at the Federal Reserve will argue that the Q.E. programs have stimulated the manufacturing sector and have thus increased American exports and American manufacturing jobs.

MY RESPONSE: This statement was essentially true several years ago. The Federal Reserve produced enough new dollars that the ever-changing worldwide value placed on the "American dollar", relative to other currencies, fell in value. The "weaker dollar" made American products overseas more attractive (less expensive) to potential buyers. American manufacturing and exports did increase for a time.

In recent years, various other countries, most notably the country of Japan have been pumping extra cash into the financial markets. Now the value of the dollar in relation to other currencies is stronger. Thus, Q.E. stimulation of American exports has substantially declined.

The new Prime Minister of Japan warned that he would not allow America or other countries to continue to devalue their currency relative to the yen. A "weak" yen helps Japanese manufacturers and exporters in the same way a "weak dollar" benefits American manufacturers selling products overseas.

In recent months, the "Central Bank of Japan" has followed the lead of America's Federal Reserve, and pumped thousands of millions of yen into the financial sector, thus causing at least temporarily, a substantial devaluation of the yen. As in America, this stimulating effort by Japan's Central Bank has resulted in immediate and rapidly increasing profits for investment bankers, brokers and active investors worldwide. Even the Central Bank of Switzerland is pumping billions of Swiss

Marks into the financial markets, in hopes of keeping the Swiss Mark from rising in value.

4. **FEDERAL RESERVE BANKERS:** Fed bankers may argue that they "have been forced" to initiate the Q.E. programs in order to stimulate the American economy in the absence of Congressional action to do so.

MY RESPONSE: Congress and the President have approved legislation specifically to stimulate the American economy on various occasions during the last five years. For example, in December of 2010, President Obama and Speaker of the House Boehner came up with a plan (that was eventually passed into law) which among other things, extended the Bush era tax cuts, extended Federal unemployment benefits and gave all Americans with earned income, a 2% cut in payroll taxes…all intended to stimulate the economy.

In addition, during the past five years, the Federal government has had a yearly deficit of over one trillion dollars. In other words, the Federal government is spending a million dollars, a million times each year in excess of the tax receipts it is receiving. Thus, "deficit spending", the rough equivalent of Federal government "charge card buying and spending," in and of itself, is a temporary stimulant for the American economy.

Even if Congress and the President were considered by Federal Reserve bankers to have insufficiently stimulated the American economy, unelected Federal Reserve bankers should have to justify their self-appointed right "to stimulate", by issuing millions of millions of extra dollars during a five year time frame.

5. **FEDERAL RESERVE BANKERS:** A primary goal of the Federal Reserve is not to make a profit but rather to implement monetary policy. Nevertheless, we at the Federal Reserve have made record profits during the last three years, most of which have been turned over to the Treasury. We turned over to the Treasury, in yearly Federal Reserve profits, $79.3 billion in 2010, $77.4 billion in 2011 and $89.9 billion in 2012.

MY RESPONSE: The Federal Reserve, since its creation has generally, year after year, "safely" turned a profit; that is, the Bank covers its own expenses and then dutifully turns over any excess profits to the Treasury. During the past five years, it could be argued, that the Federal Reserve is no longer "safely" returning a profit.

The Federal Reserve Bank, using the Q.E. programs, has more than tripled the size of its inventory of debt instruments during the past five years. By the end of 2013, current projections indicate that the ending inventory at the Fed may increase to 4 trillion dollars. Riskier debt instruments like agency mortgage backed securities are being purchased on a scale that is unprecedented in American history.

As it turns out, overall inflationary pressures, interest rates and financial market volatility have been relatively low during the past five years. Thus, the Federal Reserve Bank has been able to make large yearly profits

179

as a result of "interest earned" on its <u>massive</u> inventory of debt instruments.

However, this recent increase in yearly profitability may seem less important in the months ahead, if world-wide economic conditions dramatically decline. For example, in recent months, articles have appeared in both the New York Times and The Wall Street Journal, (which I will discuss later) that describe how the Federal Reserve could potentially suffer substantial year after year monetary losses in the face of rising interest rates.

I am not, of course demanding that the Federal Reserve be profitable or otherwise produce an adequate return on its investment in approximately 4 trillion dollars of debt instruments. I simply do not want to see the Federal Reserve lose money. I do not want to see the Federal Reserve Bank suffer <u>permanent</u> monetary losses (that exceed previous monetary profits, mentioned above) in the years ahead.

In addition, I want the Federal Reserve System to be nimble enough to handle potential future financial emergencies, particularly as they might impact the private banking system. My gut feeling is that a Federal Reserve burdened with a 4 trillion dollar inventory, is potentially less nimble, potentially less effective and potentially has fewer choices in dealing with a future financial emergency, when compared with a Federal Reserve that had only a one trillion dollar inventory figure, as was the case in early 2009.

6. FEDERAL RESERVE BANKERS: Defenders may point out that the Federal Reserve, using the Q.E. programs only purchases debt instruments that are guaranteed by the Federal government.

MY RESPONSE: As a result of such (potential) statements, some citizens may feel that the Q.E. purchases are completely safe; that is, they cannot "lose money". In reality, whether "federally guaranteed" or not, the current selling value of such debt instruments do, of course change, sometimes daily, based on economic conditions. For example, typically the price of government bonds and mortgage backed securities (which essentially are also bonds, with a mortgage used as collateral) decline as overall interest rates rise. Thus, the Federal Reserve could lose money (lots of money) if it voluntarily or is forced to sell some of its huge inventory of debt instruments in the face of higher overall interest rates.

Special Note: Most so called "debt instruments", as used in this chapter, are government bonds (or bond-like products). Bonds are "transferable" assets that require fixed payments, usually with interest, to the (bond) holder. Other examples of "debt instruments" include mortgages, notes, certificates, etc.

In addition, mortgage backed securities issued by Fannie Mae and Freddie Mac apparently do not have an "explicit" government guarantee, but rather they have an "implicit" Federal government guarantee. We can all infer that an "explicit" guarantee offers more protection than an "implicit" guarantee. For sure, at the proposed

"Grand Conference", Federal Reserve bankers will have to clearly define and explain the implications of the so called "implicit" Federal government guarantee.

7. **FEDERAL RESERVE BANKERS:** Defenders and bankers of the Federal Reserve will claim that they have stimulated the American economy during the last five years with roughly three trillion Q.E. dollars, without using "any tax payer money". They in effect have created "magic money".

MY RESPONSE: Actually, from an accounting standpoint, this claim by Federal Reserve Bankers is potentially true. Fed bankers can make this statement because technically they are getting "something in return" for the money they "pay out". They are (hopefully) not "giving away money". They are not "lending money". Rather, they are stimulating the financial services sector by "purchasing something". They are purchasing (in effect, paying out cash) for assets like mortgage backed securities and other debt instruments.

From an accounting standpoint, "cold cash" and "business inventory" are given equal status. That is, they are both considered to be assets. Business assets are typically a "good thing", business liabilities (debt) are sometimes a bad thing.

So, at the end of 2013, as a result of the Q.E. programs, you, I and the Federal government will have approximately three trillion dollars less in "potential" cold cash than we had five years ago. However, we will have instead approximately four trillion dollars' worth of (less liquid) debt instruments "piling up in the Federal Reserve basement" which draw interest and over time can hopefully be redeemed or sold.

This concludes a brief discussion of seven of the more obvious pros and cons of the Q.E. programs. The final assertion that the Fed is "stimulating" without using taxpayer money, leads nicely into discussions of the final two "under publicized" issues, referred to earlier, that Federal Reserve Bankers will have to address. These issues focus (1) on the accuracy and durability of the Fed's inventory figure of debt instruments and (2) on the overall fairness issues regarding the Q.E. programs.

SWITCHING GEARS: FOCUSING ON "LESS PUBLICIZED" ISSUES

Until now, I have discussed the more publicized arguments used to defend the Q.E. programs. Along the way I have frequently complained that the Q.E. programs have been overly beneficial to the financial services sector while short-changing the middle class. However, during these discussions, I have generally not questioned the Federal Reserve's general ability or business acumen in "carrying out" the Q.E. mandates.

Now, for the next few pages, I will "switch gears" sort of speak and raise the question of how accurate and just "how safe" is the Federal Reserve's huge inventory of debt instruments. In addition, are Federal Reserve employees adequately protecting the economic interest of all Americans as a result of their buying policies with regard to Q.E. purchases?

Since during the past five years, so many of the yearly purchases of the Federal Reserve end up in the rapidly expanding Federal Reserve's (ending) inventory, the obvious questions that every reader should be considering are these. Is the inventory of debt instruments reported by the Federal Reserve an accurate figure? Today, are the roughly 4 trillion dollars of debt instruments comprising the Federal Reserve's inventory really worth 4 trillion dollars?

How about the future? What happens to the "inventory figure" if yearly inflation rates rise substantially? What if interest rates rise (or "need to rise")? What if worldwide financial markets decline rapidly? What if the "implicit" guarantee on agency mortgaged back securities purchased by the Federal Reserve eventually became just that....implicit? What happens if the Federal Reserve is "forced" in the near future to sell part of its inventory?

If, under any of the above scenarios, the current value of the inventory of the Federal Reserve "permanently" declines (or is otherwise over stated), then the amount of that decline in inventory value represents a loss to the Federal Reserve, a loss to the Treasury, a loss to the taxpayers, but a wondrous gift to numerous hedge fund managers, private equity fund managers, investment bankers and wealthy investors somewhere in the world. In other words, the claim by the Federal Reserve that the Q.E. programs do not use taxpayer's money is only valid if the current value of the Federal Reserve's inventory is not overstated or its inventory of debt instruments is substantially durable; that is, not subject to large

184

permanent declines in the days ahead under various conditions.

Accounting rules aside, a future 500 billion dollar Federal Reserve "permanent" loss is a tax payer loss, because the "lost" money (or at least part of it) could have been, during the past five years, made available (via various Federal government and Central Bank initiatives) to working middle class citizens and middle class business owners. These groups were particularly hard hit by the financial services sector meltdown in 2007 and 2008. On the other hand, this meltdown, for sure, was partially caused by some of the various individuals and banking institutions currently receiving Q.E. money.

FEDERAL RESERVE BUYERS: ARE THEY BUYING RIGHT?

In 2008, the ending inventory of debt instruments, etc. at the Federal Reserve was a little less than one trillion dollars, but by the end of 2012, the ending inventory was roughly 3 trillion dollars. The projected inventory at the end of 2013 will be roughly 4 trillion dollars. So, obviously, most of the monthly purchases of debt instruments by the Federal Reserve are being "stored in the stock room" as ending inventory (rather than, for example, being resold or redeemed).

Thus, gauging the accuracy, durability and "overall safety" of the figures stated as the Federal Reserve inventory, will be highly dependent upon how well representatives from the Federal Reserve, are negotiating the prices actually paid for various debt instruments now and during the past five years. In other words, is the Federal Reserve getting a good deal when buying slower selling debt instruments from Goldman Sachs or other (privileged) primary dealers?

Again, readers should understand the goal of the Q.E. programs initiated by the Federal Reserve. The goal is to increase the amount of dollars circulating in the American economy's financial services sector. This goal is accomplished by in effect paying cash for various (non-cash) debt instruments, purchased from investors' worldwide (using primary dealers).

It seems obvious enough that such investment bankers and wealthy active investors are not rushing to the Federal Reserve's primary dealers to unload their best-selling, highest yielding or otherwise more valuable debt instruments. Rather, such sellers of agency mortgage backed securities and other debt instruments to the Federal Reserve are typically selling their "less worthy" debt instruments. Since the sellers of these debt instruments are getting the equivalent of cash for these "slower sellers", you would think that "buying bankers" from the Federal Reserve could "drive some pretty hard bargains" as far as what they actually pay Goldman Sachs (and their clients), for these products. As a former longtime retailer, trust me, the opportunity to exchange slower selling merchandise (or possibly any merchandise) quickly for cash is a huge (unheard of) benefit.

So at the "Grand Conference" Federal Reserve bankers need to show that they are getting a "good" or toughly negotiated price for the debt instruments like mortgage backed securities that they purchase each month. Are they paying "on average" 25 cents, 60 cents or 80 cents on the dollar for such purchases? Are they paying "full price" to primary dealers, for some of these debt instruments? Obviously, if the Federal Reserve buyers are paying 25 cents on the dollar as opposed to paying 90 cents on the dollar for such debt instruments, then we can be a little more confident regarding the durability and safety of the Federal Reserve inventory in the days ahead, just in case the value of these debt instruments permanently decline... down the road. (Incidentally, does anyone really know what the Federal Reserve actually paid for the so-called "toxic" assets (bonds) that they purchased during 2008 and 2009?)

"BUYING RIGHT": HOW WOULD WE KNOW?

The primary goal of the Federal Reserve (using the Q.E. programs) is different than the primary goal of private businesses. The Federal Reserve is "deliberately" and dramatically increasing the size of its yearly ending inventory. Most retailers and wholesalers on the other hand seek to minimize ending business inventory without sacrificing any yearly profits. This difference in "primary goals" (as it relates to inventory size) makes it difficult for those of us on the "outside" to gauge how well or how efficiently Federal Reserve bankers are negotiating with private sector bankers when buying debt instruments.

In the case of private businesses (such as retailers, wholesalers, distributors, etc.), even casual observers can reasonably gauge if the owners or purchasing agents are doing a good job of buying. For example, retailers pay wholesale prices for inventory and then try to sell the inventory at higher retail prices. If successful, then they repurchase more inventory during the year. If unsuccessful, their inventory may grow, profits shrink, and eventually the business owner may have to go out of business. After all, you cannot spend inventory.

On the other hand, accurately gauging (from the "outside") the acumen of bankers working for the Federal Reserve and buying mortgage backed securities and other debt instruments is almost impossible. Two criteria, profitability and inventory stability, that are used to gauge the success of a private business are not necessarily applicable to the Federal Reserve's operations. At the proposed Grand Conference, Federal Reserve defenders should recognize this problem and spend extra time reassuring those of us on the outside that Federal Reserve Q.E. buyers are doing a good job.

FEDERAL RESERVE Q.E. BUYERS: CONFLICTING GOALS

In a very real sense the Federal Reserve employees/bankers who are purchasing thousands of millions of dollars in debt instruments (like mortgage backed securities and other government bonds) each month have "conflicting goals". On the one hand, these bankers seek to purchase "a bunch" of debt instruments, thus maximizing the Q.E. "stimulation effect". At the same time, these bankers surely have some concern that they "protect" the government's money by not paying too much for the debt instruments purchased, which will be quickly stored in the "Federal Reserve basement".

Unless Federal Reserve bankers (perhaps at the "Grand Conference") can convince me otherwise, my "best guess" is that Federal Reserve buyers are most focused on maximizing "the stimulating effect" of their Q.E. purchases. That is, they want to purchase the full 85 billion dollars of debt instruments each month. These Federal Reserve bankers may be less concerned that the Federal Reserve is getting absolutely, positively, the very best price possible (as would be the case of most private purchasing agents) when purchasing mortgage backed securities from Goldman Sachs or other primary dealers. I base this guess on three, mostly circumstantial, criteria:

1. *NON-CONFRONTATIONAL APPROACH:* The general process of "Q.E. buying" over the past five years indicates to me a "non-confrontational approach" during the purchase of roughly $3,000,000,000,000 worth of debt instruments. For example, during the last five years the Federal Reserve has had very little problem finding sellers of Q.E. eligible debt instruments. Currently, the Federal Reserve stands ready to purchase up to 85,000 million dollars each month of debt instruments. Month after month, the Federal Reserve buys the full 85,000 million dollars of debt instruments.

It would be personally more reassuring if the Federal Reserve was occasionally only able to purchase say 56 billion dollars of debt instruments during a given month instead of the full 85 billion dollar figure, because of a general lack of sellers of Q.E. eligible debt instruments.

Similarly, I would be more reassured that the Federal Reserve was "getting a really, really good deal" when purchasing these debt instruments (again, most of which will be included in the Federal Reserve yearly ending inventory figure) if widespread complaints were heard on Wall Street and from other financial centers, that the Federal Reserve was "being unreasonable" in what it was willing to pay for mortgage backed securities, etc.

2. *HIGH INVENTORY TURNOVER:* The second reason that I "suspect" Federal Reserve Q.E. buyers are not driving a "hard enough bargain" when purchasing debt instruments is this. These "buying bankers" simply may not <u>completely</u> realize the immense economic value (to investment bankers and active investors) of such Q.E. monthly purchases of such potentially slower selling financial products. In other words, Federal Reserve bankers may not <u>fully</u> appreciate the economic value of "a high rate of inventory turnover" (that Q.E. purchases promote). Consider the following personal anecdote.

INVENTORY TURNOVER: BIG PROBLEM FOR BUSINESS OWNERS

Most retailers have a similar problem, especially middle class type retailers. There never seems to be enough cash or credit available to buy all the products that need to be purchased to maximize sales and yearly profits. Yet each day, such retailers look around their stores and see slower selling (or non-selling) merchandise. If they could quickly sell (that is "turn over") some of these "sluggish products", then the retailer might have the cash he/she needs to pay for quicker selling merchandise, etc.

Our retail stores over the years were invariably short of liquid capitol (that would be cash). In other words, my wife and I never had enough "cash on hand" to comfortably and efficiently own and operate for example, four different retail stores. Thus, we had to purchase and then price merchandise low enough that the merchandise would "turn over" relatively quickly, thus typically supplying us with the working capital we needed.

Still we always had merchandise and indoor plants that were not selling quickly enough. Thus, like all retail stores, we had various groups of merchandise marked down 20, 40 or 60% off of regular prices.

A PLANT HOSPITAL...
AT GOLDMAN SACHS?

One such group of marked down plants and extremely slow selling merchandise was always present at our stores; typically a small area in the back of the store. This area was called "The Plant Hospital". Over the years we had a goodly number of customers who would come into our stores and head straight for "The Plant Hospital". We were, trust me, very thankful for such customers.

A huge problem most retailers face is this. Even though slow selling or deteriorating products are dutifully marked down (sometimes substantially), these products may still be difficult to sell, perhaps because of a lack of "store traffic" or a general lack of disposable income among potential customers.

If before we closed our last store in 2009 (when the lease expired), a " Federal Reserve type buying banker" was visiting retail stores in the community and buying slower selling merchandise with Q.E. type cash, then our retail store would probably still be open today. A way, mystical or not, to sell, even at a sharp discount, slower moving products is absolutely huge.

Investment banking type businesses, as well as other active investors, also typically seek increased turnover of the financial products that they own. Unlike many middle class retailers, investment banking companies may not be desperate to increase inventory turnover. Yet, increased turnover of slower selling debt instruments like certain mortgage backed securities means extra profits and increased cash flow for the investment banking company.

NO NO...A TOOTH FAIRY
FOR GOLDMAN SACHS

Investment banking companies, of course, have no need for a "Plant Hospital" from which to promote their "weakest" group of debt instruments. Instead, investment banking companies have come to expect monthly visits from the Federal Reserve "tooth fairy" looking to purchase slower selling or otherwise less worthy debt instruments like various mortgage backed securities, etc.

Such purchases of "slow sellers" is a huge benefit, (more so than most readers would likely imagine) to investment bankers, for the same reason it would be a huge advantage to a middle class retailer. (Again, do you think investment bankers and wealthy active investors are rushing to the Federal Reserve, via primary dealers, to sell their faster selling, higher quality mortgage backed securities?)

The often mentioned, important point here is this. Since these Q.E. purchases of debt instruments are highly beneficial to investment bankers, then the Federal Reserve should be able to buy these assets at a very, very competitive price, perhaps at a substantial "discount off of regular price". Had the Federal Reserve "tooth fairy" visited our retail store, the opportunity to obtain immediate cash for less desirable merchandise would have encouraged me to accept 20 cents, 50 cents, or 80 cents on the dollar from the "tooth fairy", depending on the products involved. Again, the obvious question is this, are Federal Reserve Bankers (not using their own money), dealing with other private sector bankers, actually getting the very, very best deal possible for the Federal Reserve when buying mortgage backed securities and other debt instruments, especially if the rapidly increasing Federal Reserve inventory could, in fact, lose value in the months ahead?

So, as I stated to begin this section, my guess is that Federal Reserve Q.E. buyers of debt instruments do not fully appreciate the huge economic benefit to investment bankers and active investors of such Q.E. purchases. As a result, the Federal government/Federal Reserve is likely paying too much for such debt instruments. This in turn increases the chance of huge Federal Reserve monetary losses in the days ahead as described earlier.

3. *THE Q.E. PROGRAMS...ARE ANTI-CAPITAL-ISTIC:* The third and final reason, I am guessing that the Federal Reserve is paying too much for its Q.E. debt instruments purchased, is because the "buying and selling process" involved is anti-capitalistic. In other words, Federal Reserve bankers will not personally suffer "huge losses," if their Q.E. buys substantially lead to "huge losses" in the future for the Federal Reserve and the Federal Treasury.

In the real world, hundreds of millions of private commercial buyers and commercial sellers, do business each day based on the principles of free market capitalism. As discussed earlier, at the core of their activities is the opportunity to make/save money....and the possibility of "losing money".

If somehow magically, Federal Reserve bankers were collectively forced to share (over the long run) in the Federal Reserve profits derived or losses incurred as the result of Q.E. purchases of debt instruments, then I would be more reassured that such bankers were making "really, really good buys"; and thus protecting the economic interest of taxpayers (and themselves). In other words, would Q.E. buyers, over the past five years, be paying the same price for debt instruments if they were using their own money?

The four plus years of Q.E. programs are so blatantly anti-capitalistic one has to wonder why various conservative politicians, TV political pundits, and conservative radio talk show hosts have not expressed daily outrage toward the Q.E. programs. After all, $3,000,000,000 created in five years is a lot of money.

Many such individuals are prosperous or quite wealthy. Some may have large amounts of money invested in "the markets". As I have described, Q.E. stimulation has typically increased (at least temporarily) overall prices in the financial markets. Just a guess, but perhaps these "hard core" economic conservatives quietly reason that an "occasional" deter by Federal government bankers and policy makers from basic "free-market capitalistic principles" is acceptable, if this deter is temporary and its impact "minor"….as in an almost five-year long government program currently creating a million dollars, 85,000 times each month.

Q.E. BUYERS: AGAIN, ARE THEY PAYING TOO MUCH?

The three "best guesses" I have outlined, point to the argument that such Q.E. purchases can only be good buys if they fully take into account the possibility of future scenarios that would substantially decrease the value of such purchases. In other words, Q.E. buyers, in my opinion, should generally "pay less" for such financial instruments if those instruments could potentially depreciate substantially in the future.

I have further noted that my "best guess" is that Federal Reserve Q.E. buyers are <u>not</u> always making "good buys", and as a result, huge losses in the thousands of millions of dollar range are possible in the future. I could be right, I could be wrong. How do we find out? How about a "Grand Conference", the sooner the better.

FUTURE SCENARIOS...AND AN "EXIT STRATEGY"

Defenders of the Q.E. program should be able to offer an honest, fair assessment of the "potential <u>changing</u> value" of the Federal Reserve's current four trillion dollar inventory of debt instruments, under various future scenarios. In other words, in the days, months or years ahead, what happens to the Fed's inventory of debt instruments under a variety of circumstances?

As asked earlier, what happens if yearly inflation rates next year, based on the Consumer Price Index, rise to six per cent? What happens in the case of deflation? What happens if interest rates rise unexpectedly? What happens if worldwide financial markets suffer a substantial decline similar to the decline in 2007-2008? What happens if the Federal government is forced to declare that the guarantee on agency mortgage backed securities is not "explicit", but rather is only a limited "implicit" guarantee?

Also, Federal Reserve defenders will have to discuss how large they are willing to allow the "ending inventory of debt instruments" held by the Federal Reserve Bank to grow? During the 1990's, this inventory figure averaged around .75 trillion dollars. By 2008, the ending inventory figure had risen to slightly less than one trillion dollars. However, the ending inventory figure at the Federal Reserve is expected to be around 4 trillion by the end of 2013. Is it possible during the next few years that the inventory (of debt instruments) piled into the Federal Reserve's proverbial basement will exceed 6 trillion dollars? In short, what is the exit strategy of Federal Reserve bankers, or is it possible that there is... no exit strategy (despite statements to the contrary)?

THE GRAND CONFERENCE: A FEW CLUES ON WHAT TO EXPECT

During the many months of writing this book I have, until a few months ago, been unaware of many articles focusing on the "future safety" of current Q.E. purchases. However, on January 30, 2013, Victoria McGrane and Jon Hilsenrath wrote an article in the Wall Street Journal entitled "Fed Risks Losses from Bonds".

The article highlights the analysis of five Federal Reserve economists who describe how the Federal Reserve could eventually begin "losing money" each year for several years, if bonds were sold (by the Fed), in the presence of higher interest rates. The Federal Reserve economists focused on possible losses if interest rates rose to 3.8% or 4.8% and the Federal Reserve inventory was 3.25 trillion dollars or 3.75 trillion dollars.

A similar article appeared a few weeks later, on February 23, 2013, in the New York Times, entitled "Fed Officials Debate Bank's Losses Once Easing Ends", written by Benjamin Appelbaum. The article was similar to the above mentioned Wall Street Journal article in that both described the analysis of Fed economists, in which the possibility of future yearly inventory monetary losses at the Federal Reserve were evaluated.

The articles were interesting and established for me "in writing" that the Federal Reserve could lose money in the future. However, after reading the articles, my opinion is that the Federal Reserve economists were making clear that the Federal Reserve could possibly lose money, but not surprisingly, the Fed economists were not suggesting that the Federal Reserve should "change course" with regard to its current "enthusiastic" Q.E. bond buying endeavors.

Apparently, and again not surprisingly, the Fed economists did not analyze the potential negative impact of higher interest rates, say at 8 per cent or higher. Nor did these Fed economists comment on the potential negative impact to the Federal Reserve inventory of a future financial markets' meltdown, similar to the one that occurred in 2007 and 2008. (A collapse, by the way, that experts and economists at the Federal Reserve did not anticipate.) Clearly, defenders of the Q.E. programs still have many economic scenarios to consider and many questions to answer.

GONE...AND GONE FOREVER

So, at the hypothetical conference I have suggested, answers to these and other questions hopefully will successfully reassure listeners and viewers of the "future" absolute safety and durability of the Federal Reserve inventory figure. Again, this assurance can only result from Federal Reserve defenders establishing that its employees are making "good buys" with Q.E. money.

<u>We</u> <u>need</u> <u>this</u> <u>assurance</u> <u>now</u>! It will be too late, if two years from now, a "grim looking" Federal Reserve Chairman stands before a Congressional Committee and states that some of the Fed's inventory of debt instruments purchased via the "six" Q.E. programs are proving difficult to sell, given "current market conditions." The Federal Reserve Chairman may continue, "Thus, the Federal Reserve has been forced to sell some of its inventory at greatly reduced prices. The inventory at the Fed appears now to be worth closer to 4 trillion dollars, instead of the currently stated five trillion dollar figure. I am sorry, we at the Federal Reserve are currently facing economic conditions that were hard to anticipate earlier."

As discussed earlier, such a scenario would mean that some of the Federal Reserve purchases (over the years) of mortgage backed securities and other debt instruments were overpriced or otherwise "bad buys". Such a hypothetical permanent trillion dollar markdown of inventory, would mean that the Federal Reserve would have (at least) a trillion dollar permanent loss and a trillion dollars less to eventually turn over to the Treasury. Again, this potential trillion dollar shortfall would represent government funded "gifts" (not purchases) during the previous six year period, totaling one trillion dollars to a host of primary dealers, investment bankers, hedge fund managers, private equity firm managers and wealthy active investors from around the world, who successfully over the years "bamboozled" Federal Reserve buyers. The money in question would be gone and gone forever.

"WE AT THE FEDERAL RESERVE DID NOT ANTICIPATE"...BLAH, BLAH, BLAH

A successful "Grand Conference" (as proposed) could conceivably help to eliminate the possibility of this hypothetical future scenario, where a Federal Reserve Chairman justifies, for example, a 500 billion dollar permanent Federal Reserve loss on the grounds that "we at the Federal Reserve did not anticipate" the current lousy economic conditions...blah, blah, blah. Indeed, such potential future economic conditions will have already been discussed, debated and anticipated at the proposed Grand Conference.

Q.E. PURCHASES: WHAT RISK IS ACCEPTABLE?

Once the American public is adequately informed regarding the potential risk of future Federal Reserve inventory markdowns as the result of Q.E. purchases, then decisions can be reached regarding how much "risk" is appropriate. Federal Reserve bankers, some politicians, and maybe some American citizens (especially invest-ment bankers and prosperous active investors) may argue that varying degrees of risk are completely acceptable when purchasing debt instruments.

Not surprisingly, I personally think virtually "zero risk" is the appropriate guideline. For example, assume that a Federal Reserve banker is negotiating with individuals employed by one of the (privileged) primary dealers like Goldman Sachs, regarding the potential Q.E. purchase of 50 million dollars of mortgage backed securities. The eventual price paid by the Federal Reserve should be low enough that it would be almost impossible for the Federal Reserve (and the Federal Treasury) to lose money on the deal, down the road.

I understand (from experience), that all buyers occasionally make mistakes. My concern is a potential general approach by Q.E. buyers (not using their own money) that promotes Q.E. "stimulation" over tax payer "safety". Conflicting goals or not, Q.E. money, as described earlier, is potentially taxpayer money and must be protected. If this "protecting approach" decreases the Q.E. stimulating effect for prosperous investment bankers and wealthy active investors, then that would be their decision. In other words, regarding Q.E. money, an appropriate approach, in my opinion, for Federal Reserve bankers would be, "here's what I will pay, take it or leave it!"

ALREADY ON THE HOOK…
FOR FUTURE LOSSES

In the last two chapters, I have argued against the Q.E. programs. I have called for a so called Grand Conference where proponents and detractors of the Q.E. programs could in effect state their case. The problem is that such a conference should have been convened more than five years ago, before the Q.E. programs were ever initiated by the Federal Reserve. After all, such Federal Reserve programs had essentially never been used before in America and key decision makers were unelected individuals.

As it stands now, the Federal Reserve, with very little public debate, has already purchased approximately 3 trillion dollars' worth of mortgage backed securities and other debt instruments, moving into the year 2014. This 3 trillion in purchases of debt instruments may possibly have already put American taxpayers "on the hook" for billions of dollars of permanent Federal Reserve losses in the days ahead.

In addition, as noted, the Federal Reserve is currently enthusiastically purchasing 85 billion dollars' worth of debt instruments each month. So, if the Q.E. programs are more risky than generally perceived, then in order for the Federal government to cut its "potential losses" the proposed Grand Conference should be convened immediately, as in yesterday.

INFLATION: THE FINAL SAY ON INTEREST RATES

In (finally) concluding this section on the future safety of current Q.E. purchases, I would like to comment on the Federal Reserve's ability to control interest rates. The Fed chairman and other Federal Reserve bankers frequently note that the Q.E. programs help keep long term interest rates low. However, they also state that the intent of the Federal Reserve in general is to promote low interest rates several years into the future, etc.

As described earlier, one of the primary historic roles of the Federal Reserve has always been to influence interest rates. Thus, some individuals may actually think the Federal Reserve "can control" interest rates. Actually, this is not always the case. It is important to realize this fact, because my best guess is that rapidly rising interest rates pose the greatest danger to the "future" actual value of the existing Federal Reserve inventory.

The primary determiner of interest rates is not the Federal Reserve, believe it or not. Rather, "inflation", measured monthly by the Consumer Price Index, hugely impacts interest rates. In America, for example, yearly interest rates charged by lenders in the private sector will virtually always be higher than the going yearly inflation rate. Here is why.

A country's inflation rate reflects how fast the currency of that particular country is losing its value; that is its purchasing power within the country. For example, if the yearly inflation rate in America rose to say 7 per cent a year (as measured by the monthly consumer price index), then the price you pay for a basketful of groceries at the end of the year might cost you roughly 7 per cent more than the same basketful of groceries would have cost you earlier in the year,

So what banker or lender is going to lend money at a rate of 4 per cent a year, if the yearly inflation rate is expected to be 7 percent? In making such a loan, the lender would guarantee a financial loss for himself in actual purchasing power, even if the principal and interest is repaid in full. So again, interest rates in the private sector, even for the most credit worthy individuals and companies, are virtually always at least several percentage points above the going (or anticipated) inflation rates within a given country.

RISING MORTGAGE RATES: HOW ABOUT 18%?

In the very late 1970's and early 1980's, crude oil prices spiked significantly, as a result of tensions and embargos in the Middle East. As a result, crude oil (and gas prices) rose dramatically. This sharp rise in crude oil prices helped produce a sharp rise in prices for a wide array of products nationwide. Thus, the yearly inflation rate, as measured by the CPI, rose to levels greater than 10 percent during 1979, 1980 and 1981. Many experts at the time thought that yearly high inflation rates were the "new normal".

As described earlier, rising inflation rates virtually always cause an increase in interest rates. During the above mentioned time frame of high inflation rates, mortgage rates for example were temporarily close to 18 percent for highly qualified buyers. (Currently such mortgage rates are less than four per cent.)

Unlike the 10-year ongoing high crude oil prices of today, the spike in crude oil prices in and around 1980 was temporary. As crude oil prices began to fall steadily, so too did yearly inflation rates in America. Not surprisingly, this decline in inflation rates led to lower interest rates.

During most of the 1980's, all of the 1990,s and most of the years in this century, yearly inflation rates in America have been quite low, generally averaging between 1% and 3% each year. So, for roughly 30 years, the Federal Reserve has not had to deal with severe inflation as measured by the CPI. Thus, the Fed has been able to dicker with interest rates (and more recently initiate Q.E. type programs), with relatively little controversy.

Again, the simple point that I would make is this. The Federal Reserve can promote, but cannot guarantee low interest rates. Back in 2008, some experts were predicting that crude oil prices could rise to over $200 a barrel. If in fact this should ever happen, inflation could rise quickly and sharply, followed by rising interest rates. How would such a scenario affect the value of the trillions of dollars of financial instruments stored as ending inventory in the "Federal Reserve basement"?

Q.E. MONEY: THE FAIRNESS FACTOR

At the proposed conference, once the defenders and detractors of the Q.E. program have debated and established the accuracy and durability of the Federal Reserve inventory, the final point of discussion should revolve around "the fairness issue". During the past two chapters the "fairness" of the Q.E. programs has been discussed at length on numerous occasions. Simply and crudely expressed, the issue is this. Have the Q.E. programs stimulated or economically benefitted most Americans, or do the programs primarily benefit one business sector and its clients (from all over the world), while actually "hurting" the economic interests of most middle class working Americans? My position on the fairness issue is by now surely clear. Nevertheless, to recap (one more time), I see the Q.E. programs as unfair for at least three general reasons:

1. When the Federal Reserve uses the current Q.E. program to create 85,000 million dollars each month to ostensibly "stimulate the American economy," it is actually primarily stimulating the financial services sector and their wealthy active clients. The Fed purchases debt instruments from so called primary dealers, such as Goldman Sachs. These privileged banks likely sell some mortgage backed securities and other debt instruments that they already own, to the Federal Reserve buyers. In addition, hedge fund managers, equity fund managers, other investment bankers and active wealthy traders throughout America and from all over the world, can "hire" these banks to, in effect, sell their perhaps slower

moving or more risky mortgage backed securities and other debt instruments to the Federal Reserve.

Even those active investors and investment bankers who do not sell, for example, their mortgage backed securities to the Federal Reserve, typically see the selling value of their own mortgage backed securities increase, because a big new buyer has come to town, and I mean a really "big buyer." This "big buyer" of course is the Federal Reserve, currently buying $85,000,000,000 worth of debt instruments each month.

In other words, the Q.E. programs have created anti-capitalistic "artificial increases in demand" for financial products, which in turn especially benefit investment bankers, brokers and active investors. Again, whether it is the crude oil markets or the market for agency mortgage backed securities, an increase of "buying dollars" promotes increases in demand, which in turn increases prices of the given assets. (The owner and employees of Jack's Hardware Store, located many miles from a financial district, likely receive no economic benefits from these "artificial increases in demand").

IMMEDIATE DEFINITE BENEFITS
VS FUTURE POTENTIAL BENEFITS

Those in and around the financial services sector receive definite and immediate benefits from the Q.E. programs, while the vast majority of middle class Americans are expected to wait, and wait, and wait for potential benefits down the road. I understand, of course, that some middle class businesses and some middle class individuals do quickly benefit from the Q.E. programs. Middle class small businesses in and around the financial districts in big cities throughout America or middle class businesses that cater directly to investment bankers and active investors are economically benefitted. A few examples would be delis, restaurants, taxi cab companies and drivers, Mercedes Benz dealerships (and their salespersons) and other middle class businesses frequented by investment bankers and their clients. However, 85,000 million dollars each month is a lot of money. The vast bulk of that money stays in the financial services sector and typically benefits already prosperous or wealthy bankers and active investors.

Also, I understand that tens of millions of middle class Americans have retirement type IRA's, etc. that are invested in the financial markets. However, such individuals typically face restrictions or penalties if they withdraw such funds early, which have been set aside for retirement. Thus, current federal Q.E. stimulants may have little impact on the value of their retirement accounts "months or years down the road" when they retire. (Of course, tens of millions of less prosperous and middle class Americans have no IRA's, nor do they have enough disposable income to invest any money in the financial markets.)

The Federal Reserve, with the apparent (quiet) blessing of Congress and the President, has decided that it is appropriate to pump approximately one trillion dollars of Q.E. money into the financial markets during 2013. A more fair approach would be to stimulate many different business sectors and middle class individuals.

For example, the Federal Reserve could pump 300 billion dollars of Q.E. money into the financial services sector during this year and then the President, Congress and the Federal Reserve, working together, could come up with ways to use the remaining 700 billion to definitely and quickly increase disposable income of middle class citizens and businesses not directly associated with the financial sector.

2. As the Federal Reserve has pumped over 3 trillion dollars into the financial markets over the last five years, some of that "extra money" is used by brokers, active investors and other "betters" to buy commodities including crude oil. These potential "artificial increases in demand" for crude oil can cause increases in the worldwide price of crude oil, which then leads to higher gas and other fuel prices. As noted earlier, many economists agree with my oft repeated assertion that Q.E. money is potentially inflating commodity prices.

Evidently, Federal Reserve members and bankers reason that middle class citizens and business owners should be willing to pay, for example, higher prices for gas and other essential commodities now (and during the past five years) because of the potential hail storm of economic benefits that could eventually "rain down" on middle class America in the future, directly as a result of the Q.E. programs. With all due respect to America's (unelected) top bankers, to me, such reasoning is, quite simply, B.S.

3. Finally, the Federal government, using the Federal Reserve and the Q.E. programs, are quite possibly

exposing taxpayers to huge economic losses in the future, by rapidly buying trillions of dollars of "potentially risky" debt instruments. I have explained these various concerns previously.

In particular, if the ending inventory figure of the Federal Reserve is overstated, or if the Fed is "forced" to sell some of the inventory "at a permanent loss", then a portion of the Fed Q.E. stimulus money paid out to investors (using primary dealers) over the past five years could not be rightly described as "purchases". Rather any future permanent markdown of the Federal Reserve inventory (not associated with maturing debt) would represent a loss to the Federal Reserve, to the Treasury, to the Federal government and yes, to the U.S. taxpayer.

As explained earlier, money that could have been used during the past five years to "stimulate" and help increase the disposable income of working middle class families and businesses, instead will, in effect, have been paid out to tens of thousands of typically already prosperous and wealthy investment bankers and active investors worldwide. Some of these investors would have successfully sold overpriced debt instruments to the Federal Reserve. Many such recipients of these "Q.E. gifts" would be individuals and companies whose risky, callous "bets", five or six years earlier helped to cause the massive meltdown (and bailout) of the financial markets in 2007 and 2008.

In short, under a "worst case scenario", a two million dollar Q,E. purchase of debt instruments by the Federal Reserve in 2011 from a hedge fund manager (via

Goldman Sacs) living in New Jersey, could turn out to be in effect a wondrous one million dollar gift from the Federal Reserve. Part of this Federal Reserve Q.E. "purchase" could become "a gift" if the Federal Reserve is forced to sell the two million dollar Q.E. purchase (made in 2011) for one million dollars in 2014. The one million dollar Federal Reserve loss will not, of course, subsequently be repaid by our "smiling" hedge fund manager living in New Jersey. For sure, the million dollar loss/gift is gone, and…(you guessed it) gone forever. So, just how fair is that?

Special Note: I understand that during this chapter, I have not used or described many of the terms, phraseology or formats typically used by Federal Reserve bankers and private bankers from primary dealers, when buying, selling or valuing so called debt instruments. I have instead, used the "easier to understand" language and descriptions frequently used by retailers and other business owners. The problems and solutions, as described, are still completely relevant.

THE TOOTH FAIRY….
FLYING PAST THE HOUSING SECTOR

<u>Many</u> groups within the middle class need some special Q.E. type stimulation. However, for now consider the plight of one sector, the housing sector. Virtually all Americans have been negatively impacted by the incredible, almost breath-taking demise of the housing sector during the last seven years. However, relatively speaking, middle class home owners have been more negatively impacted, because historically the equity in

their homes represents a larger portion of their total net worth.

In February 2009, the Dow Jones average dropped below 7,500. At the same time the housing sector had substantially shut down. So in early 2009, both sectors were desperately short of available credit. Both sectors were in need of cash or credit injections. It is informative then to quickly review how the Federal government has dealt with the economic problems of both sectors during the last four years.

During the financial crisis of 2007 and 2008, federal policy makers in America and throughout the world turned cart wheels and somersaults to bail out investment bankers and wealthy active investors. Again, those individuals who substantially caused the economic meltdown, got "bailed out" using the money and credit of taxpayers who typically did not cause the problem…obviously, a little unfair but that is not the issue here. (We had no choice but to accept the position of powerful Federal policy makers and Federal bankers. Their claim was that in the absence of a worldwide financial services sector bailout, the economic sky would surely fall…and indeed it would have, for many, many, many wealthy active investment bankers and wealthy investors.)

The issue I am focusing on now is the Federal government response after the immediate financial crisis of 2007 and 2008 was over; that is, the Federal government response from 2009 until 2014. As I have repeatedly described, the Federal Reserve, a quasi-independent entity of the Federal government has and is, hugely subsidizing the financial services sector, principally through use of the Q.E. programs. Investment bankers, hedge fund managers, and other financial services sector businesses have typically made huge profits each quarter during the past five years...just like the old days. Currently, most stock and bond market indexes in America have reached new all-time highs...easily surpassing the record highs that were reached in 2007. (The Dow Jones average is currently trending above the 16,000 level, has established more than 50 "new highs" during 2013, and is, of course, more than double the "7,500 low point" of 2009).

On the other hand, look again at the housing sector. Not only did the housing sector not rebound after the financial crisis, the sector has actually deteriorated in most (but not all) areas of the country during the last seven years. Huge swaths of tens of millions of homes nationwide are completely void of any home owner equity. Many such houses are "underwater"...with homeowners sometimes owing the lender substantially more than their homes are actually worth.

THE "AMAZING" HOUSING RECOVERY IN AMERICA: REALLY?

In recent months, reports from the media and the Federal government loudly trumpet the fact that an "amazing" recovery is taking place in America's housing sector. Unfortunately (as you may already very well know) a closer look at the "recovery figures" indicates that much of the increases in selling prices and actual sales activity are concentrated in certain cities or in specific areas of the country.

On balance, housing prices in most areas of the country are still greatly "depressed". In some sections of the country, prices have declined by 30 per cent or more during the last six or seven years. Plus, it is difficult to sell houses in most locations throughout the country, even at these lower prices.

As a sidebar, it is interesting that some investment bankers and "active" investors, probably flush with Q.E. generated financial market profits and perhaps actual Q.E. cash, have reportedly accelerated their efforts to diversify their investments. In addition, to their portfolios of credit default swaps ("referencing" a host of riskier type bonds), their crude oil swaps contracts, their Agency Mortgage Backed Securities and a few shares of common stock, these investors and brokers have been purchasing houses (probably at substantial discounts) and have added them to their investment portfolios. Their plan, apparently, is to transform these newly purchased houses into "rental properties". Eventually, when and if the housing sector substantially rebounds, then perhaps these (active) investors will sell their houses at a nifty profit.

TRILLIONS FOR WALL STREET: LIP SERVICE FOR THE HOUSING SECTOR

The Federal government, of course, has had programs in place and has initiated several new programs during the past five years to help home owners. Fannie Mae, Freddie Mac and the FHA own or guarantee virtually all the mortgages written in recent years. Yet these policies or programs frequently benefit bankers (and, of course, active investors) as much as homeowners.

The HAMP and other similar programs were supposedly designed to help home owners having trouble making their mortgage payments. However, again such programs also help bankers and investors since it is these individuals who frequently decide who gets help from the HAMP Program and who doesn't.

Then there was the one-time "offer" of a Federal government tax credit for "first time home buyers". The so-called tax credit was actually a loan. The "credit" (if accepted) typically had to be "paid back" by such homeowners during the past several years when they filed their federal tax returns.

The group of homeowners that the Federal government has completely ignored during the past five years, is the group that is not in default or underwater on their mortgage, but is still making mortgage payments on time (sometimes with great difficulty), or perhaps simply own their homes outright. Frequently, these individuals did not substantially take advantage of the "easy money" culture existing in America from around 2001 until 2007,

Nevertheless, these homeowners, frequently middle class Americans, have seen their principal asset decline in value by up to 30 to 40 percent in some regions of the country during the past seven years. In addition, as noted, such homeowners sometimes have difficulty selling their homes even at substantially reduced prices. (Too bad these homeowners did not just rent an

215

apartment years ago and have as their primary asset, a $150,000 bundle of Agency mortgage backed securities...instead of a home. In that case the Federal Reserve, using primary dealers, would step right up and buy their mortgage backed securities. These home owners, excuse me, these apartment dwellers would then have the cash needed to buy a future home anywhere in America.)

THE AMERICAN HOUSING SECTOR:
IN SEARCH OF AN ADVOCATE

Clearly, the President, Congress, Fannie Mae, Freddie Mac, FHA, the IRS and private lenders working together and separately, could do a better job in stimulating the housing sector. I would like to offer a few suggestions. However, if I do that, then I will have to use several thousand more words to defend my suggestions. At this point, I am afraid that I have already strayed too far from the mission of this book; that is, to dramatically and quickly bring down the price of fuel all across America (and the world).

However, I will say this. The approach needed to successfully and fairly revive the housing sector is, in my opinion, similar to the approach used to revive the financial services sector. The Q.E. money pumped into the financial services sector has potentially benefitted a strong majority of bankers and investors, as the availability of credit and the prices of most financial products have risen significantly during the past five years.

Currently, the Federal government and large lenders are trying to "piece meal" and "cherry pick" certain groups of home owners to stimulate; that is, offer financial assistance. For example, consider the following "semi-hypothetical" situation. A home owner, using a 30-year mortgage, purchases a $200,000 home five years ago with no money down. He makes 36 months of payments and then decides to "strategically" quit making monthly mortgage payments on the home. Potentially, for the last two years, he will have lived in his home and made no mortgage payments. His potential savings over the two year period are likely to be twenty to thirty thousand dollars. Yet, as a result of Federal government action, this home owner may soon become eligible to have the principal owed on his mortgage actually reduced to an amount he "can afford to pay".

Again, a far better approach by the Federal government involves the entire housing sector being "stimulated" in such a way that virtually all home buyers and home sellers could potentially benefit.

IT HELPS...TO HAVE FRIENDS
IN HIGH PLACES

Hedge fund managers, equity fund managers, other wealthy active investors, as well as stockbrokers and investment bankers can smile and congratulate themselves for "fighting and clawing" their way out of the 2007/2008 financial collapse. But they should also ask themselves, where would they be right now without the more than $3,000,000,000,000 (3 trillion dollars) of Q.E. money deposited in their bank accounts during the past five years via the Q.E. programs? Hint: take a look at the housing sector and the economic plight of most home owners.

Find a way to pump 3 trillion dollars (over a 5-year period) into any business sector in America and those associated with the sector are going to do quite nicely. So, again my point is this. The Federal government and the Federal Reserve working together or separately should be more fair and even handed in deciding who "gets stimulated" and who does not.

THE GRAND CONFERENCE: CHANGING MY MIND?

It is fair to say that I have serious reservations about the Q.E. programs. However, it is possible that Federal Reserve bankers can change the opinion of skeptics like myself. That is one reason why the proposed conference in my opinion is so necessary.

If, on the other hand, it becomes abundantly obvious at the Conference that the Q.E. programs are, or could soon prove to be, a huge mistake, then the gut instinct of some skeptics might be to "round up more donkeys and purchase more feathers". Unfortunately, solving the Q.E. problem (if there is a problem) is not that simple.

Even if it becomes abundantly clear that the Q.E. programs are a risky mistake, the current Q.E. programs could not be immediately discontinued. In other words, if the Federal Reserve Board Chairman held a news conference next week and announced "after further review" that the Federal Reserve had decided to immediately discontinue the current Q.E. program (which pumps 85 billion dollars into the financial services sector <u>each</u> month), then financial market indexes in America and around the world would very likely drop in one day by 3 to 5%.

In other words, in one day the Dow Jones Industrial average could fall by 500 points or more. Such a potential (but very realistic) drop in value illustrates just how addicted many stock brokers, investment bankers and wealthy active investors (worldwide) have become during the past five years to Federal government or Central Bank economic stimulation and/or bailouts.

Readers who have the time can go to the computer and track the major stock market indexes of the world. Such individuals will discover that during the last five years virtually all of the "major swings", up or down, in the worldwide financial markets (pretty much in unison) were the result of (or the anticipation of) a Federal government or Central Bank (somewhere on the planet) deciding to stimulate or otherwise economically bail out investment bankers and the active wealthy investors of the world.

ENDING AN ADDICTION....SLOWLY

Instead of quickly and completely eliminating Q.E. stimulants, the Federal Open Market Committee would likely have to end the current Q.E. programs more slowly. It could take perhaps three to six months to gradually phase out the current program. Even so, wealthy "active" investors, investment bankers and brokers are not going to be pleased.

Compared with other industrialized countries in the world, America's Central Bank, the Federal Reserve, has been, during the past five years, more aggressive regarding stimulation of the financial services sector (with Q.E. type programs). However, during the past several years, many other central banks, like the European Central Bank, Bank of England, Bank of Japan, even Switzerland's Central Bank have also become more aggressive in stimulating financial sectors (or bailing out debt ridden countries and the investors who have lent these countries money via sovereign bond purchases).

For instance, the European Central Bank buys the sometimes risky sovereign bonds of countries like Spain, Italy, etc. In so doing, the Central Bank buys the slower selling, impossible to sell or otherwise risky sovereign bonds from typically prosperous or wealthy bankers and active investors. In return for these dubious sovereign bonds, investment bankers and investors receive fresh crisp new euros…to probably go out and buy more risky sovereign bonds, etc.

WELL…WHERE'S MINE?

Special note: During the worldwide financial bailout of 2007 and 2008, and during the past five years, over and over we hear phrases used like, "financial services sector bailout", "bank bailouts", "Wall Street bailouts", "worldwide banking system bailout", bailouts of companies like AIG or bailouts of countries like Greece or

Spain. However, though a "company", a "country" or an "institution" is bailed out, in the end it is individuals (fellow human beings) like equity fund managers, hedge fund managers, investment bankers or active wealthy investors, who typically receive (immediate) cash benefits.

These individuals time and again during the past five years have been on the verge of losing vast sums of money. In most cases these individuals had purchased high yield, but risky type sovereign (or corporate) bonds, betting (correctly) that even if the bond issuers could not "make good" on the bonds, then tax payers, a large commercial bank, a Federal Reserve type bank, the International Monetary Fund or some other lending institution, after much (supposedly) "wringing of the hands", would eventually "buy up" or otherwise make these "questionable bonds" whole.

In other words, such investment bankers and wealthy active investors have apparently perfected a very lucrative business model. For example, they buy risky government bonds from Italy, collect high interest rates on these dubious bonds for a while and then, if and when the bonds become increasingly worthless….BINGO in flies a beautiful tooth fairy with all the euros, yen, dollars or marks that are needed to put smiles on the faces of all the shrewd active investors involved. In addition, she simultaneously saves the Euro, the European Union and the World's commercial banking system, as well as promoting world peace, feeding the hungry, clothing the naked, curing obesity, etc., blah, blah, blah.

So, yes, if you the reader, are currently or have been in recent years, under economic type duress, then you have every right to look your favorite politician or Federal Reserve banker in the eye and say, "where the heck is mine?"

RITALIN FREE... FINANCIAL MARKETS

If the American Federal Reserve decides to reduce and then end Q.E. stimulation of the financial markets, then it is quite possible that the governments and government central banks in other countries will similarly slow down or end their "buy back", stimulating or otherwise "bailing out" type programs for investment bankers, brokers and wealthy active investors. This potential worldwide decline in special treatment for active wealthy investors and bankers would of course be initially painful.

Such active investors, together with the investment bankers and brokers of the world, frequently controlling thousands of millions of dollars of investment grade capitol, will likely personally drive financial market indexes temporarily lower worldwide. Nevertheless, weaning big time investors from five years of government "handouts" is likely the best first step of a potential four-step approach to return sanity (and reality) to the financial markets in America and around the world.

This approach would force active investors and bankers to return to classic, less leveraged, more conservative principles in evaluating the risk of various financial products and the earning potential of millions of corporate stock and bond offerings. In addition, slowly deflating (what appears to be) a worldwide "financial markets bubble" now, is preferable to having the bubble "pop" or rapidly deflate in the months ahead.

If indeed fuel prices decline and stabilize world-wide, and these lower prices continue for years into the future, then virtually all companies listed on stock exchanges throughout the world (with the exception of oil companies and those companies that service or cater to the oil industry, as well as investment banking companies focusing on crude oil speculation) would potentially become at least a little more profitable very quickly.

In addition, hundreds of millions of middle class individuals and small businesses in America and also in economically hard pressed countries like Greece, Spain, Italy, etc., will potentially become more profitable or a little more prosperous. This increased disposable income and prosperity should provide increased tax revenue for these currently economically weakened countries and perhaps allow them to do a better job of paying their bills (without bailout money from Federal or commercial banks).

"STOCK MARKET" TURN-AROUND: ONLY QUESTION, HOW QUICKLY?

So significantly reduced and stable gasoline prices will increase the disposable income of hundreds of millions of individuals in communities worldwide. (The only possible exceptions may be individuals living in countries who rely heavily on crude oil exports; countries like Russia, Iran, Venezuela and various Arab countries). Most small and large businesses throughout the world will become more profitable. Countries that are currently economically hard pressed will, as described, be in a better position to manage their debt obligations. Such factors are typically "good for business" and ultimately good for most investors.

Thus, in the end, these "<u>real</u>" positive economic factors (all promoted by significantly lower oil and fuel prices) will offset the loss of "artificial" factors (like Q.E. dollars, "magic money" produced by the central banks of various countries, bailout cash and tons of petro dollars) that are currently inflating the worldwide financial markets' bubble. At some point, hopefully sooner than later, such positive economic factors will encourage a <u>true</u>, widespread, long term "uptick" in stock and bond prices worldwide. However, this is simply a personal opinion. I am not an expert concerning, nor am I invested in, the financial markets.

QUICK REVIEW: ONE VERY LAST TIME

Before moving to the next and final chapter, here is a quick and final review of the key points of this book. First and foremost, I am asking you the reader to join me in petitioning your elected Representatives and demanding of them four separate guarantees:

1. A guarantee of a complete ban on crude oil (and gasoline) speculation

224

2. A guarantee of adequate competition between crude oil producers

3. A guarantee that Federal Reserve bankers, along with their defenders and detractors, will be forced to <u>highly</u> publicize and openly debate (for the benefit of the uninformed citizenry) the positives and the potential negatives of the Q.E. programs, perhaps using the "Conference format" that I described earlier.   My <u>guess</u> is that such a conference will result in the "scaling back" or elimination of the Q.E. programs, while at the same time spotlighting the need for Q.E. type stimulation in other sectors of America's economy.

4. A guarantee that new federal initiatives will be proposed, debated and voted upon by Congress that could potentially quickly increase disposable income of tens of millions of middle class families. Such initiatives, as described, could help restart the "job creating machines" in communities throughout America. This book's proposed Federal government initiative to ban crude oil speculation, thus potentially bringing down gas and other fuel prices, stands as a fitting example of how creative Federal policy makers, if the will is truly there, can come up with initiatives that increase monthly disposable income for virtually all Americans; but relatively speaking, positively impacting middle class and less prosperous families the most.

As I mentioned earlier, I can think of other government initiatives that would quickly increase disposable income for millions of middle class citizens and that would eventually benefit virtually all American families and businesses. In fact, I am currently working on another short book describing in detail an additional federal initiative to immediately increase middle class disposable income. Perhaps you personally can think of such initiatives as well. Remember, all "worthy" and original political thought and ideas do not necessarily originate in front of TV cameras or from behind radio microphones.

TWO STEP, THREE STEP, OR FOUR STEP PLAN: DOES ANYONE CARE?

What I have outlined in the previous chapters is this. The first five chapters outline a "two step plan" to bring down gasoline prices, including (1) a "ban on crude oil speculation" and (2) "forcing oil companies to better compete". In Chapters 8 and 9, I argue that "a third step" may be needed to maximize the reduction of crude oil and gasoline prices. That step requires that the Federal Reserve end (or greatly reduce the size of) the Q.E. programs. Thus, our "two-step plan" to reduce gasoline and other fuel prices would probably be more accurately described as a "three step plan".

Beyond the plan describing how to bring down gasoline prices, I have argued throughout the book of the need to improve the "economic lives" of middle class citizens. In particular, Chapter 7 discusses in some detail, an actual "plan" that would increase middle class disposable income and potentially begin a widespread American economic recovery.

So in the end what this book is promoting is a "three step plan" to bring down fuel prices and a "four step plan" to dramatically improve the economic lot of middle class America. The "four step plan" would include the three "fuel price reducing steps", plus a fourth step, which would promote additional federal initiatives to increase middle class disposable income.

CHAPTER TEN

CONGRESS: WILL THEY COOPERATE?

Even if you the readers agree that the "four-step plan" outlined in the previous pages is indeed "worthy", how do we then get Congress to do its part? The President and most Congressional members are not going, at least initially, to enthusiastically support, for example, a complete ban on speculating in the crude oil markets. Many, many generous campaign contributors engage in this frequently very profitable business activity. Ditto: Congressional members confronting oil company executives or Federal Reserve bankers.

SPECIAL INTEREST GROUPS VERSUS MIDDLE CLASS AMERICANS

All politicians claim to have an undying allegiance to the economic welfare of middle class citizens (and of course, small business owners). This concern is real. The economic well-being of the middle class citizenry hugely impacts who gets re-elected. Unfortunately, most politicians also feel that they <u>must</u> have the financial support of wealthy citizens and generous special interest groups. Conventional wisdom dictates that winning re-election in America requires a lot of money; that is, typically requires many generous campaign donors.

Thus, Presidents and Congressional members, Democrats and Republicans alike, (as well as their defenders in the media) spend a goodly amount of time contemplating and implementing strategies/policies to keep both groups of individuals (that is, middle class citizens and wealthy campaign contributors) happy. The simplest and most used approach by these politicians is to simply "ignore", if possible, potential legislation which could benefit the middle class if that legislation might in fact put frowns on the faces of large campaign donors.

Another favorite tactic of Congressional politicians and Presidents is to cobble together legislation (sometimes dealing with a simple straight forward problem) that it is so lengthy, and its provisions and regulations so complex, that even many experts, let alone average middle class citizens, do not understand their political impact. Good examples would be Obama Care and the Dodd/Frank Financial Reform Act.

Still another "smoking mirrors" type tactic used by Congressional members and Presidents, is to approve (frequently complex) legislation where many of the provisions or rules of the legislation are to be determined later, sometimes years down the road. Again, Obama Care and the Dodd/Frank Financial Reform Act are good examples.

So, we have come full circle. As the article in Chapter One points out, Congressional members sometimes ignore obvious, simple and less expensive solutions to problems that are economically hammering middle class families and middle class small business owners, because such solutions are unpopular with financially generous campaign donors. That is exactly the situation we have before us right now. Congressional members simply could do much more to economically help middle class America.

For example, Congress could act to potentially bring down fuel prices almost immediately by "banning" crude oil speculation. Most members are, after all, not stupid. This potential, relatively simple solution, is the equivalent of the proverbial "dead elephant in the room". However, proposing such a complete ban (or challenging the competitiveness of oil producers), would anger many wealthy campaign donors. That is why we have to force the issue; force Congressional members to debate and take a stand. That is one of the purposes of this book.

PARTISAN ELECTORATE...
PARTISAN CONGRESS

Besides the problem of Congressional favoritism directed at generous campaign donors, a second perhaps more serious problem exists that could slow down our efforts to make $1.25 gas a reality. The problem is this. Most experts agree that the recent Congressional delegations are unusually partisan and unproductive, even by Congressional standards.

Every word and every vote of many Congressional members seems to have one purpose: be deliberately partisan, toe the Democratic Party line, establishment Republican Party line or "Tea Party" Republican line...and thus supposedly increase chances of re-election in November.

However, as explained in a moment, a partisan Congress; that is, Congressional members trying to be "good Democrats" or "good Republicans", can be overcome. But first, the citizenry will have to overcome the same tendency.

Middle class and less prosperous Americans need to understand that occasionally an initiative is proposed, like the one outlined in this book (to bring down gas prices), which without question, hugely benefits economically the vast majority of small business owners and middle class families, be they Democrats or Republicans. In such situations, constituents could temporarily ignore their allegiances to a particular political party, and its spokespersons. Instead, such constituents could think for themselves and focus on petitioning their respective Congressional members to pass "the middle class initiative," period!

Whether a middle class individual is a Republican or Democrat, conservative or liberal, black or white, Christian or non-Christian, pro-life or pro-choice, union worker or non-union worker, privately or publicly employed; such individuals should come together on the initiatives I have outlined in this book. After all, there are middle class Republicans and middle class Democrats who have worked hard all of their lives, yet frequently during the past five or ten years, have seen their personal dreams and those for their children economically crushed. It is time for a change...not President Obama type change, but real change. The initiatives outlined in this book (to lower gas prices and quickly help economically rejuvenate the middle class) are just such "real changes".

Similar Federal initiatives that immediately and definitely benefit middle class families are very possible. However, if middle class Republicans and Democrats cannot come together in support of these relatively uncontroversial initiatives to lower gas prices, then bi-partisan support from the electorate for similar "Federal government initiatives" in the future might be lacking as well. Thus, widespread bi-partisan support now is crucial.

Ideally, the initiatives outlined in this book (to lower gas prices and benefit the middle class) will gain such overwhelming support from the electorate "back home" that the leaders from both political parties in Washington might "see the handwriting on the wall". These leaders just might feel led "to co-sponsor legislation" promoting the middle class initiative in question; for example, a ban on crude oil speculation. Co-sponsorship by members of both political parties would decrease the chances that passage of the legislation would offer a political advantage to one political party over the other.

ALL THINGS POSSIBLE...WHEN
DEMOCRACY REIGNS

All things are possible in a Republic founded on true democratic principles. A partisan Congress can become non-partisan, if a partisan electorate can temporarily become non-partisan. This is a fundamental premise that has prompted the writing of this book. I firmly believe that if enough of us petition our elected representatives regarding any relevant issue or cause, the impossible (practically speaking) becomes very possible.

If one million citizens contact the President and their respective Congressional representatives, demanding "a ban" on crude oil speculation, then these policy makers will take note. What if ten million, maybe twenty million, make contact? At some point, enough political energy is created that the President and Congressional members definitely feel the heat. In other words, a federal politician's tendency toward partisan politics and quietly paying "special attention" to the wishes of powerful, well-funded, generous special interest groups will evaporate, if enough political heat is generated. I think it was President Reagan (and perhaps others) who said, in effect, that if "the people" generate enough political heat, then politicians will suddenly see the light.

In the days ahead, if a politician or political pundit tells me that "practically speaking" or "realistically speaking", there is absolutely no way that Congress is going to actually consider and debate, for example, our three step plan to reduce crude oil prices, I will simply respond, "Is that a fact". Then I will set out to promote the message that "all things are possible".

To be sure, the question of "practicality" is not the major problem we will face in the days ahead. The primary problem will be "ignorance". Congressional politicians and other defenders of crude oil speculators, big oil companies and the Q.E. programs will try to completely "ignore" the existence of this book and its plan to lower gas prices. If we reach the stage where Congressional members are accusing me of being naïve or unreasonable, then as described earlier, we are well on the way to winning the battle; the battle for dramatically lowered fuel prices. In other words, publicity is everything. Publicizing the three step plan is huge.

In conclusion, regardless of my critics, every idea put forth, every problem described and every solution offered are original and/or based on truth, as best that I understand it. I stand behind the book 100%.

Beyond that, the important point is this. Regardless of the merits of the previous pages of print, this book does outline a potential solution (that could be implemented almost immediately) to a very serious problem in America; that is, the problem of high and unstable fuel prices. To the best of my knowledge, as hard as it is to believe, no other such immediate solution has been offered or well publicized that could quickly and dramatically reduce and stabilize fuel prices. Thus, if our plan is "the only game in town", then perhaps we need to run with it for better or for worse.

So, I am "all in" regarding a complete ban on crude oil speculation, demanding realistic and verifiable competition between oil producing companies and promoting the notion of a complete and public review of the Federal Reserve's Q.E. programs. I am, of course, willing to defend this book at any time. However, for now I have done what I can do. The rest is up to you. If you get involved, we get low gas prices and a true middle class economic recovery. If you don't, we won't.